A SHOWER OF ROSES

A Shower of Roses

*The Most Beautiful Miracles
of Saint Thérèse of Lisieux*

BY CAMILLE BURETTE

ARCHIVIST OF THE CARMEL OF LISIEUX

Translated by Sr. Marie of the Child Jesus
Foreword by ✠ Jacques Habert,
Bishop of Bayeux and Lisieux

Angelico Press

First published in French as
Pluie de roses
Les plus beaux miracles de Thérèse de Lisieux

© 2023, Éditions de l'Emmanuel; 89, Bd Auguste
Blanqui – 75013 PARIS (France);
ISBN: 978-2-38433-124-6
© Archives du Carmel de Lisieux, 2025
© Angelico Press, 2025

For information, address:
Angelico Press, Ltd.
169 Monitor St.
Brooklyn, NY 11222
www.angelicopress.com

Ppr 979-8-89280-105-8
Cloth 979-8-89280-106-5
Ebook 979-8-89280-107-2

Book and cover design
by Michael Schrauzer

To my dad

CONTENTS

FOREWORD

IN THIS DOUBLE YEAR OF JUBILEE (OF HER BIRTH and of her beatification), books on Saint Thérèse of the Child Jesus are becoming more and more numerous. One can only be pleased with it. All of that literature demonstrates, if there were a need, the popularity of the greatest saint of modern times. Yes, Thérèse is still loved and prayed to. Pilgrims who go to the shrine of Lisieux every year amply demonstrate it; and it is always impressive to see they come from all over the world.

This book Camille Burette offers us is captivating. The author emphatically reminds us how well Thérèse kept her double promise:

> "I will spend my heaven doing good on earth."
> "I will let fall a shower of roses."

Camille Burette has had the privilege of serving for years as the archivist of the Carmel of Lisieux, where a unique and precious resource is available to her. In the present book, she selected accounts from dozens of miracles performed by Thérèse since—and even before—her beatification in 1923. Her selection represents only a tiny portion of all the miracles inventoried, which probably themselves represent only a tiny portion of those actually performed.

When faced with the question of miracles, we Christians of the twenty-first century are sometimes hesitant. We don't want to be credulous; we want to understand, to justify, to verify. This prudence is not in itself unhealthy. The rigor of those who work in the Office of Medical Observations[1] in Lourdes demonstrates it. The same goes for the thorough work done in order to recognize a miracle in canonization processes. Yes,

---

[1] The office in charge of scientifically investigating claims of miraculous healings—trans.

the Church is prudent; she doesn't want to deceive people.

But the Church also knows she must leave the Lord free to do as He pleases. The *Catechism of the Catholic Church* explains it this way: "Whatever their character—sometimes it is extraordinary, such as the gift of miracles or of tongues—charisms are oriented toward sanctifying grace and are intended for the common good of the Church. They are at the service of charity which builds up the Church" (no. 2003). Thérèse, in heaven, continues to exercise her charisms; she thus contributes to building up the Church. The accounts of miracles here related are quite consistent with the Gospel. We often find the same pattern: a person's (or a group of persons') faith, a simple and pure act of faith, and peace that surpasses all understanding.

This book allows us to make a real journey through history. The stories related to World War I are deeply moving. But we also stay in the present era of the Church's life. Some stories are from the current century. As the bishop of the diocese of Bayeux and Lisieux, I have noticed that some letters from catechumens directly allude to Thérèse's mysterious presence in their conversion process. This book also enables us to make a journey through space. We travel across all the continents with her who wanted to go to the end of the earth.

Here is a book that can comfort us. May this year of jubilee encourage us all to immerse ourselves in the captivating and demanding adventure of Saint Thérèse's "Little Way." Thérèse is our sister, she accompanies us on the sometimes chaotic pilgrimage of our Christian lives. She leads us on a way of confidence and abandonment to God. May this work be a source of hope and comfort to all.

✠ Jacques Habert
Bishop of Bayeux and Lisieux

The Martin sisters in Carmel
Top: Sister Marie of the Sacred Heart (Marie)
and Sister Geneviève (Céline)
Bottom: Mother Agnès of Jesus (Pauline) and Thérèse

INTRODUCTION

"I want to spend my heaven doing good on earth."
"After my death, I will let fall a shower of roses."

THESE ARE CERTAINLY THE MOST FAMOUS WORDS
of Saint Thérèse of the Child Jesus. Thérèse pronounced
these sentences at the end of her life, when she was suffering
from tuberculosis and was about to "enter into life."[1] Many
times, she explained to her sisters and to her relations that
she "firmly intends not to remain idle in heaven."[2]

It is to be noted that in her day, the idea of being still
active on earth after one's death wasn't widespread at all. But
Thérèse desired it deeply. From March 4 to 12, 1897, she did
the "novena of grace" to Saint Francis Xavier, the patron
saint of missions; at that time, she confided to Sister Marie
of the Sacred Heart (her elder sister Marie): "I asked for the
grace of doing good after my death and now I'm sure to be
answered, because one obtains through this novena all one
desires." On the following March 19, the feast of Saint Joseph,
she went to the Saint Joseph Hermitage with the intention
of asking him to support that request to Saint Francis Xavier.

On June 9, 1897, Sister Marie of the Sacred Heart told
Thérèse that the sisters would deeply grieve after her death.
She replied: "Oh no! You will see, it will be like a shower
of roses."[3] Marie explained in her testimony at the ordinary
process how Thérèse got the idea of letting fall a "shower
of roses." She related: "I had read at the refectory a fact in
the life of Saint Aloysius Gonzaga, saying that a sick man
requesting to be healed had seen a shower of roses fall onto

---

[1] Letter of June 9, 1897.
[2] Letter of July 14, 1897.
[3] *Last Conversations.*

his bed, as a symbol of the grace he was to receive. 'I too,' she then told me during recreation, 'will let fall a shower of roses after my death.'"[4] The phrase "a shower of roses" has referred ever since to Thérèse's miracles.

On July 17, 1897, Thérèse, who had been in the infirmary for a few days, explained to Mother Agnès of Jesus (her sister Pauline, the second of the Martin sisters, who were five in total) what her action in heaven would consist in: "I feel that I'm about to enter my rest.... But above all I feel that my mission is about to begin, my mission to have the Lord loved as I love Him, to give my Little Way to souls. If the Lord answers my desires, my heaven will be spent on earth till the end of the world. Yes, I want to spend my heaven doing good on earth. It is not impossible, since even within the beatific vision, the angels are looking after us. I'm not enthralled by the delights awaiting me in heaven, I can't rest as long as there remain souls to be saved.... But when the angel will have announced: 'Time is no more!' then I will rest, then I can enjoy heaven's delights, for the number of the elect will be complete, and all will have entered into joy and rest. My heart is thrilled with this thought..."[5]

What Thérèse wanted was "to have little children baptized, to help priests, missionaries, the whole Church..."[6] And it wasn't long before she manifested herself on earth. But how did she do it? What exactly are the "miracles" in question? According to a dictionary, a miracle is an "extraordinary event in which it is believed a benevolent divine intervention took place, to which some spiritual significance is assigned." There

---

[4] At the time, the ordinary process was the first part of the enquiry of the process of beatification. It was followed by an apostolic process.
[5] *Last Conversations.*
[6] Idem.

is nothing "magical" in the stories that will be related here. The supernatural events people were favored with mostly resulted from fervent and confident prayer. Such miracles are granted with a specific aim, for example to incite their recipients to turn to God, to pray more, to show humility or charity. In brief, through her miracles Thérèse wants to induce them to follow her "Little Way" of confidence and love that will bring them closer to the Lord, and to bring them along with her on the way of faith.

In the Bible, the miracles performed by Jesus are often determined by the faith and cooperation displayed either by those favored with them or by their relatives. Moreover, "when Jesus heals, the Father actually is the one acting through him."[7] When we pray to Thérèse, she's not the one directly performing the miracle, rather she intercedes for us before the Lord, who alone can perform miracles.

But before she could intercede for a multitude, Thérèse had to make herself known. It was through the propagation of her autobiography, *The Story of a Soul*, that she became famous and the renowned "hurricane of glory" began—a phrase used by Pope Pius XI to refer to the incredible quantity of miracles and graces received through her intercession in the beginning of the twentieth century. Printed at a thousand copies as early as 1898, one year after her death, *The Story of a Soul* was first given out to the 121 French Carmels and to 18 foreign Carmels, as well as to the local clergy, to serve as a "circular," which is to say an obituary. Very soon, this work, which one of the Carmelites of Lisieux thought was only good to wedge the furniture, was hugely successful. Many

---

[7] Alain de Bloudemande, "Les miracles de Jésus dans l'Évangile" (Jesus's miracles in the Gospel), in *Il Est Vivant!*, no. 344, March 3, 2020, https://emmanuel.info/miracles-de-jesus-evangile-iev-344.

readers were touched by the words of the young Carmelite, who would enjoy more and more fame by word of mouth. A thousand additional copies were reprinted very quickly; a second edition saw the light of day as soon as May 1899. Editions then came in succession at a rate of one every year or two. The total number is currently estimated at more than five hundred million copies around the world.

Many, after reading *The Story of a Soul*, invoked Thérèse and were answered. Some of them spoke of the book, lent it out, or handed out images and relics to those around them. Thérèse's promise to "do good on earth" was written down as a reminder on the cross of the cemetery, where pilgrims were beginning to come and pray, so much so that very soon, as Thérèse had announced to her sisters, the Carmel's letterbox was filled with mail. She had indeed predicted: "After my death, when you'll go pick up the mail, you'll find consolations there!"[8] In her testimony at the ordinary process, Mother Agnès of Jesus explained that favors granted by Thérèse "have become countless" and that "the daily correspondence that reaches [her] from all over the globe contains the accounts of a great variety of graces; some less important, others quite prodigious." On the advice of Monsignor De Teil, vice-postulator of the cause of beatification, she preserved all these letters and published them.

Already in the 1907 edition of *The Story of a Soul*, sixty-six of these graces were included in a section named *Pluie de Roses* (A Shower of Roses), in memory of the phrase used by Thérèse. In March 1910, an 82-page collection listing 167 miracles, titled *Pluie de Roses*, was published. This little pamphlet was sold at the price of fifty centimes. At the end of the book could be found a prayer for Thérèse's beatification.

---

[8] *Last Conversations.*

Between 1913 and 1926, seven volumes of *Pluie de Roses* were published. The publication was temporarily interrupted after the fourth volume, while the second process, known as the apostolic process, was taking place (1915–1917). When it came out in 1920, the fifth volume was all the more abundant, rich in Thérèse's interventions on the battlefield during World War I.

The Carmelites' collaboration with artist Charles Jouvenot made it possible to produce attractive illustrated volumes. Moreover, accounts of about forty miracles and interventions were set to music in order to accompany screenings of these drawings. It was possible to rent glass or celluloid plates at the Central Office of Lisieux, 102 pictures in total representing miracles, for the purpose of viewing them, and to buy the musical score. Lastly, small-format booklets sold at a modest sum made it possible for everyone to have access to the accounts of miracles according to his budget.

Thus, numerous ways were devised to introduce the public to the powerful intercession of Thérèse, and as a result speed up her cause, for miracles are required in order to recognize the sainthood of a Servant of God. They are subject to a "canonical procedure on the reality of the miracles" during which several cases are studied by expert physicians, by the promoter of the faith, who submits objections, and by defense advocates. At the time, two miracles were necessary for beatification, and two others for canonization.

While the publication of *Pluie de Roses* stopped in 1926, miracle stories kept appearing in the *Annales de Thérèse de Lisieux*, the shrine's magazine that later became *Thérèse de Lisieux*, in a dedicated section that still exists today. The present book aims to continue this editorial tradition.

The Carmel of Lisieux keeps in its archives more than

13,500 miracle stories, from 1899 to today. Since not all of Thérèse's miracles are impressive healings of incurable illnesses, less strong words than "miracle" are sometimes used to refer to them: "favors," "graces," or "interventions." The graces granted are very diverse. While healings represent more than half, we also find conversions, spiritual graces, protections amidst dangers, assistance for academic or professional success, and assistance in family life, friendship, social life, and psycho-affective life, as well as material and economic assistance. These favors are sometimes accompanied by phenomena such as the perception of perfumes, apparitions of Thérèse, or the sound of her voice.

Readers will find in this book a large range of moving, impressive, or even funny miracles, for Thérèse can be surprising. Some are well known, such as the miracle of Gallipoli; others were already published in the *Pluie de Roses* volumes or in the *Annales de Thérèse de Lisieux*; but many are still unpublished. All eras are represented, from the early twentieth century to today, for Thérèse is still active in heaven and doesn't intend to stop anytime soon!

World War I

WHEN WORLD WAR I BROKE OUT IN AUGUST 1914, Thérèse was already known in France and in foreign countries through the publication of *The Story of a Soul* and its first translations, but also by word of mouth. A list of numerous miracles and graces obtained through her intercession was already circulating; pilgrims flocked to Lisieux, especially to the Carmel, to the cemetery, and to Les Buissonnets, her childhood home. But Thérèse's fame was about to skyrocket thanks to her many interventions in favor of the *Poilus*[1] on the battlefield.

Much of Thérèse's beatification process took place during the war. After the opening of the ordinary process in 1910, Pope Pius X officially introduced the cause on June 10, 1914. As for the apostolic process, it was opened on March 17, 1915, and then handed over to Rome after its closing in the cathedral of Bayeux on October 30, 1917.

In 1915, the Vatican allowed medals bearing the image of Thérèse, then only a "Servant of God," to be issued. Many were the soldiers who, before they departed for the front, slipped a medal or a relic of Thérèse into their wallet. Since society at the time was undergoing significant dechristianization, they were not necessarily all believers. Some would sometimes reluctantly wear them, to please their mother or their spouse. Others already had great confidence in the little Carmelite after reading her life, usually in its abridged version. On the front, her fame increased very rapidly, and images representing the famous charcoal drawing *Thérèse with Roses* were given out by chaplains, by nun-nurses, or by the most zealous soldiers.

---

[1] Nickname of the French soldiers during World War I—trans.

Thérèse with Roses
A charcoal by Sister Geneviève of the Holy Face, 1912

In the mail from the *Poilus* we come across many affectionate nicknames given to Thérèse: she was their "little sister of the trenches," their "war godmother," "the fighters' favorite," "the *Poilu*'s saint," "the soldiers' shield," or "the angel of battles." For some, she was already considered a "little saint." We mustn't forget that Thérèse herself was from a family of military men. Her maternal grandfather, Pierre-François Martin, was an infantry captain and a knight of the Order of Saint Louis; he took part in the Spanish Campaign in 1823–1824. As for her maternal grandfather, Isidore Guérin, a policeman, he fought for ten years in the Napoleonic wars. The military world was already familiar to Thérèse, and she didn't hesitate to incorporate its vocabulary into the spiritual life in her writings, as in her poem *My Arms*.

During the war, soldiers on leave would often go on pilgrimages to Therese's grave to ask for her protection or to thank her for the graces they had obtained. These were diverse, and granted to French as well as to German men. Thérèse brought protection, healing, encouragement, comfort, or conversion. Some soldiers were even favored with an apparition. In the rear, women also went to her grave to leave there prayer requests and photographs of their husbands or sons.

Besides letters, the Carmel also received numerous *ex-votos*, objects offered in gratitude for graces received. They show us the diverse crafts of the trenches. Shell cases carved with roses, picture frames made of ammunition, rings manufactured with the aluminum of German rockets and bearing the engraved image of Thérèse, or sculpted oak leaves: many of these artworks made a stone's throw from the fighting, in makeshift shelters. Soldiers also sent their medals, war crosses, or Légions d'Honneur.[2] Banners from different countries were also received.

In 1916, Officer Pierre Mestre, commander of the 9th Battalion of the 92nd Infantry Regiment and friend to the Carmel, had the idea of sending Pope Benedict XV petitions of soldiers asking for Thérèse's canonization. Father Emmanuel Bailly, general superior of the Assumptionists, offered to bring these requests to Rome. They recounted the diverse graces received in the trenches, and demonstrated the fame Thérèse enjoyed among French soldiers. This era unquestionably represents the starting point for Thérèse's "hurricane of glory" that would spread all over the world.

THE BATTERY "SISTER THÉRÈSE OF THE CHILD JESUS"

Private Paul Dugast, aged 26, was a gun pointer[3] in the 51st Artillery Regiment. After the general draft of August 1, 1914, he joined his regiment on August 3, and marched off to the front as early as August 10. His family placed him under the protection of the Virgin Mary and of Thérèse, whose relic he wore.

In the beginning of September, during the battle of the Marne, his regiment found itself facing the enemy with only eight cannons against twenty-five, and lacking ammunition. When the fire ceased, in his haste he fell down and had his legs crushed by his cannon, which weighed almost two tons. His comrades hurried to his assistance.

---

[2] Legion of Honor (*Légion d'Honneur*): the highest French order of merit for military and civil merits—trans.

[3] Literally *maître pointeur*: the distinction of maître pointeur was officially awarded to particularly gifted and experienced artillery pointers; there is no equivalent in English—trans.

Much to their surprise, Paul got up unscathed, so that they all exclaimed: "Miracle! Miracle!" Paul Dugast replied to them: "I owe this protection to little sister Thérèse of the Child Jesus!" He immediately pulled a white pencil out of his pocket and wrote on the cannon in big letters: "Battery Sister Thérèse of the Child Jesus." Later on, in a letter to his grandmother, he told her that if the rain ended up erasing this writing, he would write it again as soon as possible.

In December 1916, the Carmel wrote to Paul Dugast's family to inform them he wished to buy a small cannon to be placed as an *ex-voto* in Thérèse's cell, with the name Paul Dugast on it. The family contributed 2 francs.

IN THE MIDDLE OF A MARCH, THE WOUND ON HIS LEG WAS SUDDENLY HEALED

In the beginning of the battle of the Aisne, on September 16, 1914, Fernand Ducom, an engineer and a corporal in the 2nd Engineer Regiment, Company 19/2, was about to go on a long march. He was exhausted by combat and his right foot was seriously skinned, to the extent that he couldn't wear his shoe any more. Taking the image of Thérèse, he applied it on his wound "with the greatest confidence," then put on his shoe and set off again. A few moments later, he perceived his foot was soaked and felt no more pain. He recounted: "Within five to six minutes, right in the middle of the march, my wound had healed! I checked it as soon as I could. The limb was perfectly sound and bore no trace of the injury. Obviously, the fatigue of this painful day couldn't have brought about this sudden healing; humanly speaking, it ought to have delayed it, on the contrary. But the hand of the little saint had touched me!"

THÉRÈSE LIFTS UP A WOUNDED SOLDIER ON THE BATTLEFIELD

Private Roger Lefevbre, from the Bernay region, in Eure,[4] was part of the 224th Infantry Regiment. Aged 28, he was married, and a father to two boys, aged three and one. A staunch believer, he also had unlimited confidence in Thérèse, whom he invoked more than twenty times a day, and whose relic and image he permanently wore.

When World War I broke out, he was sent to La Neuville, near Reims. On Thursday, September 17, 1914, at half past four in the afternoon, while the fight was raging and the shells were pouring in, Roger Lefebvre passed out. Seriously wounded by six pieces of shrapnel, he had been struck in his head, in his face, in his thigh; he had a dreadful gash in his foot; and the veins of his neck were cut. He regained consciousness in the middle of the battlefield in the cool of the evening, covered in his own blood, which kept gushing from his open wounds. Feeling so faint he might die, he cried out: "My sister Thérèse, come to my rescue!" Immediately afterwards, he saw her appear before him, holding a large crucifix in one hand. She took him by the right arm, lifted him up, smiled, and disappeared. At this instant, the blood suddenly stopped flowing out and he didn't feel pain any more. He ran to a first-aid station located 400 meters (almost 450 yards) away from the battlefield. While he was being treated, his pains didn't come back, even though he was operated on without anesthesia for the gash in his foot.

Fully recovered, he went to Lisieux with his wife on February 4, 1915 to thank Thérèse at her grave, as he had vowed to do. On the following July 15, he met the prioress, Mother

---

[4] Eure is one of the administrative departments of Normandy, Saint Thérèse's native region—trans.

Agnès of Jesus, whom Thérèse called her "little mother," in the Carmel's parlor, and related to her with emotion and simplicity what had happened to him. He told her: "I wish all non-believers had such an apparition! I didn't know whether I would live or not. It's enough to change a man's mind. I told everyone I could what had happened to me. You see, my heart is still leaping when I think about it!" When asked if the Little Thérèse was beautiful, he replied: "Oh yes, she is beautiful! Much more beautiful than in her images. It's as if I were still seeing her." Mother Agnès then asked him: "Now that you are healed, will you go back to the front?" He replied with enthusiasm: "Oh yes, Sister, I soon will, and I assure you that it will be without fear, for my sister Thérèse, who protected me once, will protect me always!"

He also asked for relics "to convert my comrades and do them good." At least one of them would later acknowledge some supernatural protection through contact with Roger. "Is he the one who protects us all? I have no idea. What is certain is that before he arrived at the front, we had nine men killed and a good many wounded in the company within three days. Since he has been with us, not a single one has been harmed!"

In November 1915, his wife gave birth to a little girl whom he named Thérèse. Roger Lefebvre kept in touch with the Carmelites and regularly sent them news from the front. He liked to call himself "Thérèse's Protégé."

On June 1, 1916, a worried Mrs. Lefebvre wrote to the Carmel to report that her husband was either dead or a prisoner in the wake of the attack of Fort Vaux[5] by the Ger-

---

[5] Located near Verdun, the fortress became a symbol of victory for the French army after the Germans failed to take it in November 1916, thus losing the important Battle of Verdun — trans.

mans during the battle of Verdun. After five days of intense bombing, an assault was launched during the night of May 31, during which 1,200 combatants died or went missing. Still protected by Thérèse, Roger Lefebvre escaped with his life. Wounded, but not seriously, he was taken prisoner by the Germans and transferred to a military hospital in Stuttgart.

When the chapel of the reliquary was built in 1923, one of the stained-glass windows representing various miracles of Thérèse was devoted to his story and is still visible in the Carmel's chapel. Still in touch with the Carmelites in 1943, Roger Lefebvre mentioned he went on a pilgrimage to Lisieux every year.

Roger Lefebvre's story was the subject of a little book handed out to soldiers to introduce them to Thérèse.

THÉRÈSE APPEARED TO HIM AND ENCOURAGED HIM

Private André Pelletier, of the 43rd Colonial Infantry Regiment, although a lukewarm believer who didn't go to Mass, visited Lisieux with his wife in July 1914. His cousin took them to the Carmel's chapel and then to Thérèse's grave. She gave Mrs. Pelletier a photograph of Thérèse as well as a little relic: a piece of her casket's wood. On this occasion, the soldier heard Thérèse had promised to spend her heaven doing good on earth, and he took note of the miracles worked through her intercession.

The next month, war was declared and André was drafted. His wife gave him Thérèse's relic, "with all the confidence that has always filled her," and urged him to pray to her often. She taught him a very short but fervent prayer. During the battle of Morhange,[6] on August 19 and 20, 1914, he lost his relic on the battlefield, but came out unscathed. At the end of September, he left the east for the north, and reached Maricout, in the Somme.[7]

On September 30, 1914, at twilight, around seven in the evening, his company was heading for the Maricourt wood when it was blocked by shells of all calibers shot by German

---

[6] One of the first battles of World War I, fought in Lorraine, one of the French regions partially annexed by the German empire in 1871—trans.
[7] A department in northern France, known for the eponymous World War I battle—trans.

artillery. Thus faced with great danger, he commended himself to Thérèse and asked her to protect him. At the same time the order was given to go forward at any cost. This is when he saw before him, high in the sky, a nun "positioned before a window." Thinking he was hallucinating, he briefly closed his eyes, then opened them again: the nun was still there. At that moment he recognized Thérèse, "first of all from her angelic smile." She encouraged him with her eyes, then waved to him, which he interpreted as an exhortation to confidence, courage, and hope. She was wearing a cloak, as in her portrait. He closed his eyes again. When he opened them, she had disappeared, leaving him under the impression of having seen something celestial and unforgettable, and from this point on feeling stronger and more protected.

André Pelletier hadn't known September 30 was the anniversary of Thérèse's death. He learned about it later on, when he read *Une Rose Effeuillée* (A Rose Unpetalled), her abridged biography. According to his parish priest, Father Charles, this apparition restored Private Pelletier's faith. The latter wrote that it gave him "belief, confidence, and salvation."

Céline Martin, Thérèse's sister, is indirectly involved in this story, for on the very same September 30, around the hour Thérèse had "entered life," she decided to go up to the attic and scan the horizon in quest of a sign from her little sister, sure that on this special day she "would perform some sign to guide the troops."[8] She saw nothing at the moment, but remained full of confidence. Eight months later, in June 1915, she received a letter from Father Charles informing her of this apparition, which had taken place at the very hour of Thérèse's death.

---

[8] Testimony of Sister Geneviève of the Holy Face (the name of Céline in religion) during the apostolic process.

Sergeant Marcel Dutoit

On October 10, 1914, Marcel Dutoit, sergeant in the 10th Company of the 8th Territorial Infantry Regiment, was in the rearguard of the 3rd Battalion, which was going back to Lille. The company soon found itself surrounded by the German cavalry, without cannons or batteries. As a non-commissioned officer, he was especially vulnerable to enemy fire: three machine-guns were pointed at him. Hit by a bullet in his upper thigh, he fell into a ditch full of water by the side of the road, near Armentières. Unable to move, he expected to be taken prisoner by the Germans, but after twenty minutes, much to his surprise, French farmers came and lifted him up, and took him to their farm. They hid him in their barn with two horses. A few minutes later, German soldiers came into the farm and searched it, but failed to find the sergeant.

He thus remained hidden in the barn for a whole week. Many times, sometimes up to ten times a day, the farm was searched by the Germans, but Marcel Dutoit was never found. He wrote: "I was absolutely convinced that Sister Thérèse was guarding me, and I didn't fail to invoke her at each new attempt. I even seemed to see her before the door, guarding its entrance."

One day, when he seemed about to be discovered, he begged Thérèse to "avert this extreme danger." Suddenly, he saw these words written in white letters above the door: "Don't be afraid, you will be saved." The German soldiers inspected the barns nearby, but not the one he was hiding in. A week later, he was taken in by an English patrol and out of danger.

HE DIED COMFORTED BY A VISION OF THÉRÈSE

Joseph Fresneau caught typhoid on the front. After suffering for three weeks, particularly from headaches, he remembered that his mother had given him a relic of Thérèse. He placed it on the painful areas and obtained immediate relief. He then wrote to his mother: "You see, dear mother, you must reassure yourself and have confidence, as I have, in Sister Thérèse."

The soldier eventually succumbed to his illness on November 9, 1914, but on the eve of his death, around seven or eight in the morning, the priest-nurse who was taking care of him saw him stretch his arms and utter these words: "Oh, how beautiful she is! There she is! She is inviting me to go with her..." Once his vision had disappeared, he confided: "Father, I just saw the little sister Thérèse."

CELESTIAL SEDATIVE

In December 1914, Sister Saint-Alphonse, of the Sisters of Saint Charles in Lyon, related Therese's intervention on behalf of two soldiers hospitalized in Néronde, Loire. The first, aged 20, was suffering from accute inflammation in his arm as a consequence of a wound. Excruciating pains had been preventing him from sleeping for two weeks. The sister put a relic of Thérèse under his pillow and recommended that he pray to her and have confidence. He smiled and whispered: "Ah! How glad I would be if she only would make me sleep!" A quarter of an hour later, he fell peacefully asleep. Waking up three times in order to drink, he said: "I don't know if your saint is the one who's making me sleep, but I'm feeling pretty well!" Through this Thérèse ended up earning the nickname "celestial sedative" from the nun.

Another soldier, afflicted with meningitis because of a bullet that had gone through both ears, was suffering horribly and couldn't sleep either. The same relic produced the same effects, and consequently saved him as well from certain death: on the following day the medical officer declared him out of danger.

"BE BRAVE! YOU WILL SOON BE HOME."

At the beginning of January 1915, a Mrs. Sans started a novena to Thérèse, requesting her help in some family dispute. She asked her to manifest herself to one of her relatives. The only person who could settle the issue, however, was a nephew, at the time mobilized at La Rochelle. On the fifth day of the novena, at night, the nephew was woken by a hand striking his feet. Thinking it was his roommate, he snarled: "Now what?" But much to his surprise, he saw Thérèse at his feet. She told him: "Be brave! You will soon be home." He knew nothing then of the novena done by his aunt. On January 14, he was declared unfit for service, and the following day he came back home, which allowed him to settle the family problem.

FROZEN FEET HEALED

In the trenches of Argonne, in early February 1915, Private Louis Tanguy was suffering from frostbite. His heels especially were affected and were entirely black. The medical officer had him evacuated. His pain was so intense that he couldn't stand a single blanket on his feet. Seized with compassion, a nurse introduced him to Thérèse and gave him a relic and a picture, assuring him she would heal him if he prayed to her with confidence. After hearing this he began a novena. On the morning of the fourth day, he felt no more pain. He removed the bandages wrapped around his feet and observed they were completely healed.

"A ROSE FROM PARADISE"

Private Léon Vandamme, aged 25, had fallen ill on the front on October 18, 1914. Suffering from asthma and neuralgic pains in his heart, and utterly exhausted, he was evacuated to La Panne in Belgium, then to Calais and to Cabourg, before finally arriving in Caen on November 3, and eventually, in that city, ended up on February 27, 1915 at the community of Le Bon Sauveur,[9] where Louis Martin, Thérèse's father,

---

[9] A large mental hospital held by the Daughters of the Good Savior (*Filles du Bon Sauveur*), a congregation of hospital nuns—trans.

was received during his last illness twenty-five years earlier.

On the day following Léon's arrival, one of the sisters gave him *The Story of a Soul* and a relic. From this point on, the soldier invoked Thérèse several times a day for his healing. After reading that she had said, "After my death, I will let fall a shower of roses," he also asked her to send him a rose from paradise, to prove the healing really came from her.

On May 30, 1915, at 11 p.m., still awake, he had a vision: "I clearly saw the Blessed Virgin Mary before me, and a few seconds later, a Carmelite nun appeared by her side, wearing a white cloak. Oh, how beautiful she was! She was holding in her hands a basket of roses and tossed one onto my bed with a smile. Then they both disappeared and I fell asleep. Sadly, when I woke up I didn't find the rose, but on the morning of May 31, I was healed."

A few years later, he went on a thanksgiving pilgrimage to Lisieux and prayed in the Carmel's chapel. He was very impressed to see the statue of the Virgin of the Smile placed above Thérèse's shrine: it was exactly like the Virgin who had appeared to him.

HIS HORSE FOUND HIS LOST RELIC

In March 1915, Lionel Delafoy, a young artilleryman, received a relic of Thérèse from his brother, Father Guy Delafoy. Shortly after receiving it, he lost it on the battlefield. Although this loss saddened him greatly, he could see no way to find it again. On the following day, he was riding down the battlefield when, suddenly, his horse stopped, moved his head, and stomped vigorously. In spite of the soldier's spurring, he refused to go forward. He insistently plunged his head deep down, three times in a row. Not understanding his horse's obstinacy, the gunner got off his mount and inspected the ground, trying to find what was frightening it. He bent down, and near the horse's hoof he caught sight of his "precious relic."

SAVED FROM DROWNING BY THÉRÈSE

One day in March 1915, around 10 p.m., Private Joseph Derrien was walking through the countryside with several brothers-in-arms in the vicinity of Anzin-Saint-Aubin, Pas-de-Calais. Finding himself some thirty yards away from his comrades, in the darkness, he was unable to see and couldn't find his way. Catching sight of something brighter he mistook for a road, he put his foot down. But it was actually a deep river, the current of which was very dangerous. He sank straight to the deepest spot, unable to swim. Feeling lost, he cried out: "My sister Thérèse, come to my rescue!"

Right away, without any effort, he felt he was being placed on the bank of the river. He then ran to his comrades, soaking, and explained his misfortune to them. When they saw the spot of his fall, the other soldiers couldn't believe he had escaped alone without any external assistance. Not saying a word, Joseph Derrien thought: "It's a miracle, sister Thérèse was the one who saved my life."

MAILWOMAN THÉRÈSE

Eugène Cailleaux, a stretcher-bearer in the 5th Company of the 33rd Infantry Regiment, was hospitalized in Aix-les-Bains in June 1915. With no news from his family back in occupied territory, he made two novenas to Thérèse, requesting that he would hear from them. During the second, Thérèse appeared to him. He recounted: "I saw Sister Thérèse all dressed in white, it was a real vision; she showed me five letters, one after another, saying to me: 'Look.'"

She disappeared immediately, and Eugène couldn't find the letters she had placed by his side. On the following morning, during the mail delivery, he received the five letters she had announced.

THÉRÈSE COMFORTS A PRISONER OF WAR

Taken prisoner in Maubeuge on September 8, 1914, Private Édouard Dekonne was sent to the prison camp of Friedrichsfeld, Germany. One evening in June 1915, he went to the chapel and fervently asked Thérèse that he not be sent to work in the factories of Germany. On coming out, he was overcome by a strong smell of roses, the perfume of which remained for half an hour, though neither a garden nor flowers were to be found nearby. "In this way, the little saint wanted to assure me she had heard my entreaties," he said.

On the following day, he was summoned to a medical checkup. Without even examining him, the doctor classified him as ill and sent him to Switzerland, although he was perfectly well, while many soldiers, sometimes with worse health, were selected to go to the factories.

A PIECE OF SHRAPNEL STOPS AT THÉRÈSE'S PICTURE

We find in the archives of the Carmel of Lisieux several testimonies recounting how a picture, a relic, or a book of Thérèse stopped a potentially lethal bullet or piece of shrapnel. Sometimes the lacerated picture was placed in the envelope with the letter, as a proof of the impact's violence. Private Madoux was one of those who benefited from this special protection granted by Thérèse.

Like many soldiers' mothers, Mrs. Madoux requested from the Carmel a picture and a relic of Thérèse for her son Léon before he went off to the front, and commended him to the

Carmelites' prayers. On August 24, 1915, he was in Berry-au-Bac, Aisne. Around 10 a.m., done with his guard duty in the trench, he was about to take some rest, when suddenly a 77-millimeter German shell exploded two meters away from him. His friends rushed to him right away and asked: "Léon, are you not wounded?" He replied: "No, I have nothing, I was only dazed." "But Léon, can't you see? There is a hole in your jacket!"

His jacket indeed had a hole, level with the heart, pierced by a piece of shrapnel. In his pocket was his wallet, inside which all his papers had been torn by the shrapnel. All except one: the image of Thérèse had remained intact. In a letter to his mother, he affirmed: "I do believe that the good sister protected me; at any rate I pray to her diligently every day."

THANKS TO THÉRÈSE, HE SAVED EIGHT GERMAN PRISONERS FROM DEATH

Sergeant-major Joseph Durier, of the 99th Infantry Regiment, discovered Thérèse two years before the war, while he was in Mexico. There he received an image of the young Carmelite nun, which he never tired of gazing at. On the image he read: "I would like to love Jesus so much," and, "I want to spend my heaven doing good on earth." And he said to himself: "What a saint! But how on earth can she be interested in me?" An inner voice replied to him: "In the family of the good God, all the members love and help each other without any distinction of families or countries, and looking down from heaven, the saints take a keen interest in those who invoke them." From that day on, he recited the prayer to obtain Thérèse's beatification every night. In November 1914, right before going to the front, a friend to whom he had never confided his devotion to Thérèse gave him a relic. His devotion increased even more, and he commended himself to her every night.

In September 1915, during the Battle of Champagne, the signal for a new attack was given. Right before it, he kissed the image of Thérèse and pressed her relic against his heart. While most of his comrades were shot down, he escaped unscathed. A bullet suddenly went through his greatcoat and his trousers, level with his left thigh, without even grazing his skin. He related: "I immediately recognized my saint's protection, and to thank her, I saved the life of eight German prisoners my men were about to send before the Supreme Judge."

THE SIGHT OF THÉRÈSE'S PORTRAIT LIFTS UP THE SPIRITS OF A DESPONDENT SOLDIER

In 1916, shortly before the Battle of Verdun, a young soldier, deprived of news from his family and traumatized by the "horrible carnage" he had been witnessing since the beginning of the war, was completely despondent. At that time, he received an image of Thérèse. He related: "With my mind in disarray, I took that sweet image as my only refuge, and courage came back to me. Full of absolute confidence in my new protector, I went emotionless through the most intense bombardments and the most horrible German attacks; I even received a decoration and a citation, the content of which I take the liberty of communicating to you, to better show you to what extent the saint had lifted up my spirits: 'Took part in all the perilous missions; volunteered for a liaison mission during a violent barrage.'" The soldier later sent his Croix de Guerre[10] to the Carmel.

---

[10] A French military medal.

Private André Lévesque was part of the 102nd Infantry Regiment and had been on the front since October 1914. He constantly wore a medal and a relic of Thérèse. His parents had told him of the miracles she performed and urged him to invoke her, especially in case of danger.

On March 12, 1916, he found himself in a trench with four comrades, when 150-millimeter shells, "that is to say shells with a diameter of 15 centimeters [6 inches], and 45 centimeters [18 inches] long," fell down on their shelter. At that moment, André prayed: "Little Sister Thérèse of the Child Jesus, watch over me as you always have." One moment later, a big shell fell down on the soldiers' hut. It smashed the roof open and ended up stuck in the ground, almost under their feet . . . but didn't explode. André explained that "if it had exploded, we would not even have been found." They all were thrown to the ground; two of his friends were wounded in the leg because beams had fallen on them, but not seriously. As for André, he was unscathed. He wrote to the Carmelites: "The protection of Sister Thérèse is too obvious not to say it is a true miracle. For this reason, during our rest days I received Holy Communion in thanksgiving and can never thank her enough; it is my duty to publish it."

"GET AWAY FROM HERE"

A non-believing sublieutenant went to war, reluctantly agreeing to wear a relic of Thérèse and promised never to get rid of it. It happened that on the day of an important battle in 1916, while he was looking through the periscope, he heard a sweet voice telling him: "Get away from here." He didn't pay attention to it, but the warning came a second time, and then a third. He eventually decided to leave his place, not really understanding why. A few moments later, a shell crashed to the spot where he had been. Realizing this mysterious voice had saved him from certain death, he converted and wished to become a good Catholic: "I now believe in God, and I owe it to Sister Thérèse," he wrote to his family.

SAVED FROM A WAR DOG'S ATTACK

Côme Camélio, of the 3rd Heavy Artillery Regiment, discovered Thérèse through the intervention of a chaplain who gave him her image. He took it to the front. On the evening of Pentecost, June 11, 1916, he experienced her special protection. While he was joining his encampment near Arras, alone on the road, he was attacked by a big enemy war dog, trained to attack French soldiers. Bitten on his left leg, he was not armed and thus could not defend himself against this dog, which wouldn't let go. Full of confidence, he invoked Thérèse. The dog immediately loosened its mouth and ran away with a muffled growl.

HE SAW THÉRÈSE'S STARRY "T" AND WAS PROTECTED BY IT

Shortly before her husband's departure for the front, Mrs. Bernard gave him a relic of Thérèse. He was reluctant to take it, thinking he already had enough medals. On the eve of his departure, his wife saw Thérèse's "T" in the sky,[11] "so wide, so beautiful, as [she] had never seen it before." She showed it to her husband, telling him she was now certain

---

[11] It is an allusion to the stars of the constellation of Orion, about which Thérèse related: "I watched the sweetly scintillating stars and this sight ravished me.... There was above all a group of golden pearls which I noticed with joy, finding that it had the shape of a 'T'; I pointed it out to Papa, telling him that my name was written in the sky."

he would be protected. He finally agreed to take the relic, and then received Communion before going off to the front.

One day in January 1917, around ten at night, he was ordered by his lieutenant to take command of the 9th battery and leave the position he had been occupying for one month. To do this he had to cross a bridge that was often bombed by the enemy. Right when he was about to step onto the bridge, shells began to pour down around him. At that moment he invoked Thérèse and asked her to protect him and his men. The barrage immediately stopped, allowing them to cross the bridge without danger. He then lifted his eyes heavenwards to thank Thérèse, and saw her "T" among the many stars.

"I TELEGRAPHED SISTER THÉRÈSE!"

Father Marius Julienne was a priest of the diocese of Bayeux and Lisieux, and a teacher at Sainte-Marie high school in Caen. When the war broke out, he became an aircraft mechanic in the V 109 squadron. On October 29, 1917, during a flight, the motor of the plane stalled. Tossed by the wind, the plane crashed violently into the ground.

Much to the surprise of the officers and of the soldiers who had rushed to the spot of the accident, the three occupants of the plane came out unscathed, while the craft itself had been pulverized. Father Julienne explained he owed this happy ending to the intervention of Thérèse: "Having foreseen the catastrophe, I telegraphed Sister Thérèse of the Child Jesus to come to our rescue, and it wasn't in vain."

Grateful to his protector, the priest sent to the Carmel of Lisieux a piece of his plane's propeller as an *ex-voto*. He also named after her the first plane he blessed afterwards, the crew of which survived many dangerous expeditions.

Father Marius Julienne (center)
and his crew before the *Sister Thérèse*

"IT IS I, LITTLE SISTER THÉRÈSE"

Private Pierre Albert wrote to the Carmel on November 2, 1918 to recount how Thérèse got him out of a perilous situation. On the previous day, while he was on the side of the road during "one hell of a bombardment," he was thinking about Thérèse, when a shell suddenly fell down close to him, knocked over his machine gun, and buried him underground. Feeling he was in great danger, he called on Thérèse for help. He first heard her voice telling him not to move, and that nothing would happen to him. He then felt her hand taking his, and very gently, she helped him to extricate himself. Eventually he saw her before him, and she told him: "It is I, little Sister Thérèse."

Healings

THE MARTIN FAMILY WAS NOT SPARED TRIALS and sickness. In 1865 Zélie Martin noticed a lump in her breast which turned out to be a cancerous tumor. She passed away from it on August 28, 1877, after great suffering. As for Louis Martin, he suffered from cerebral arteriosclerosis with flare-ups of uremia, a disease that caused him to lose his mind. After yet another attack on February 2, 1889, he was committed to Le Bon Sauveur Hospital in Caen, where he remained for three years. Thérèse was confronted with her father's illness when she had just entered Carmel. To the pain of knowing he was ill was added that of not being by his side. Louis Martin passed away as a result of a serious heart attack on July 29, 1894.

Four of the nine Martin children died of illness in early infancy, much to the sorrow of their parents. Thérèse herself wasn't spared either. Aged two months, she suffered from enteritis and had to be entrusted to a wet nurse. Aged ten, she suffered from her "strange illness," which forced her to be confined to bed, the victim of dreadful hallucinations, from March 25 to May 13, 1883. Subsequently, her father had a novena of Masses said at Notre-Dame des Victoires,[1] through whose intercession Thérèse was healed on May 13, 1883, after seeing the "ravishing smile of the Blessed Virgin." Tuberculosis finally carried her off on September 30, 1897 after causing her dreadful sufferings.

---

[1] Notre-Dame des Victoires (Our Lady of Victories) is a church in Paris, where Our Lady appeared in 1637 to a Capuchin friar, to reveal to him that an heir to the throne of France would be granted at last, which later prompted King Louis XIII to consecrate France to Our Lady. At the time of Louis and Zélie Martin, the church was the headquarters of a popular archconfraternity dedicated to the Immaculate Conception, to which the Martin family was deeply devoted—trans.

Since Thérèse had promised to spend her heaven doing good on earth, she was very soon invoked for healing. As a matter of fact, the very first copy sold of *The Story of a Soul* caused the healing of its owner. Healings represent more than half of the miracles reported to the Carmel. Moreover, the miracles acknowledged in Thérèse's beatification and canonization are exclusively healings, for they are the only easily "provable" ones, by means of medical reports.

Ex-votos sent to the Carmel and placed in the dormitory leading to Thérèse's cell (second door)

MIRACLES ACCEPTED IN THE BEATIFICATION

The first miracle acknowledged in Thérèse's beatification was that of Sister Louise of Saint Germain, a nun in the convent of the Daughters of the Cross, in Ustaritz, Pays Basque, healed in 1916 from a lethal, hemorrhagic stomach ulcer.

The second miracle was that of seminarian Charles Anne, from Lisieux, healed in 1906 from galloping pulmonary consumption.

Marie-Renée Lauroa, in religion Sister Louise of Saint Germain, joined the Daughters of the Cross in Ustaritz in 1911, at the age of 23. During her novitiate in 1911–1912, she began to regularly experience stomach- and headaches, along with vomiting. However, this prevented her neither from taking her vows nor from going to Spain as a primary-school teacher just after her religious profession.

In May 1913, the pains became more frequent, and her regular vomiting of blood showed that an ulcer had formed in her stomach, up to the duodenum. Back in Ustaritz for treatment, she was put on an appropriate diet and on complete rest. After a more acute attack on November 14, 1915, she stayed in the infirmary for eight months, after which she was authorized to go back to Spain.

On May 28, 1915, the symptoms came back, "along with abundant hemorrhaging." An operation was becoming necessary, but was impossible because of the patient's extreme weakness and anemia. Sister Louise was sent back to the provincial house of Ustaritz. During the journey her condition got worse, so much so that upon arrival, she was administered the last rites. For thirty-two days, she remained in a state of total exhaustion, consuming only a few mouthfuls of ice water, regurgitated at the cost of "acute suffering giving [her] the sensation of being lacerated or stabbed, in [her] stomach as well as in [her] intestines." Ice was permanently kept on her head and on her stomach.

From June 3 to 11, the community began a novena to Thérèse, joined by Sister Louise. On July 1, around 3 a.m., Thérèse appeared to her and told her: "Recite faithfully everyday three *Pater Nosters*, *Ave Marias,* and *Glorias,* and three times the invocation 'Sacred Heart of Jesus, protect the

Church, France, and the Congregation.' Spread this devotion among your sisters."

The next day and two days later, Thérèse appeared to her again at the same hour, repeating the same words. On the morning of July 3, she gently put her hand on Sister Louise's head to reassure her. During these three days, a mysterious scent filled the room with no possible natural explanation. Sister Louise wrote: "The illness continued, however. I was still praying to Sister Thérèse, but without asking for my healing; submitted to the will of the good God, I was offering my sufferings for the intentions recommended by the saint." For one more year, she experienced alternate periods of attacks and of respite.

Sister Louise of Saint Germain

In early September 1916, Sister Julie Germaine, who was visiting, advised her to repeat her prayers to Thérèse: "Therefore I did it, adding to prayer many acts of virtue, so that just like Thérèse, I could touch the Heart of Jesus by offering him my little sacrifices."

On September 10, bedridden after an attack, she was favored with an apparition of Thérèse, who told her: "Be generous. You will soon recover, I promise you." Thérèse then disappeared. On the following morning, the three nuns sleeping in the infirmary found rose petals of all colors at the foot of Sister Louise's bed.

On September 17, Sister Louise had a bad attack. Vomiting, hemorrhaging, and syncope succeeded each other for five days. On September 21, after a severe final attack, she fell asleep around 9 p.m., only to wake the following morning around half past five . . . completely healed. "No more pain, and a sensation of general well-being persuaded me the disease had disappeared. Only weakness and hunger made themselves felt. I joyfully got out of bed to ask permission to go and attend Holy Mass." "Out of wise prudence," the superior forced her to stay in bed, but had food brought to her. She first had coffee with milk, which she digested perfectly well, and then bread for a second breakfast around half past seven, and at ten a glass of milk. During the day, she had two additional hearty meals in the infirmary's refectory without any problem, even eating meat, which she had not done for five years. For several days, out of precaution, she followed the sick sisters' diet—broth, white meat, eggs, wine, and cheese—and digested everything normally.

According to Doctor Le Bec, who examined her case, "Among these foods, some are absolutely incompatible with ulcer, namely: coffee, wine, and solid foods such as meat and bread. For this food of the first day, as well as that of the following days, to be tolerated, the ulcer would have had to completely disappear between the evening of September 21 . . . and the sister's awakening, around half past five in the morning, which means within a span of six to seven hours at the maximum. In clinical medicine, however, we have never seen things progress at such a rapid pace. The healing of an ulcer always takes place extremely slowly; it usually takes months."

This miracle was acknowledged in the beatification for several reasons. First of all, the illness was proven. Sister Louise was presenting the four symptoms of ulcer, namely stomach pains, food vomiting, blood vomiting, and alternate periods of calm and attacks. Also there is no way the "time factor" played a part in the healing: it was far too rapid to be of natural origin, and happened after a bad attack of symptoms. Lastly, the healing persisted. At the time of the beatification, Sister Louise had been healed for seven years and had experienced no relapse. X-rays showed no more trace of the ulcer and her blood tests were good.

Seminarian Charles Anne

Charles Anne entered the seminary of the diocese of Bayeux and Lisieux in October 1903 at the age of 19. In June 1905, he coughed up large amounts of blood for the first time, and saw Doctor La Néele about it during his holiday in Lisieux. The latter happened to be a cousin by marriage of Thérèse, whom he had treated during her last illness. Back in seminary in 1906, Charles coughed up blood again, and developed a fever that lasted six days. Taken back to his parents' house, he was treated by Doctors La Néele and Loisnel, who noticed the presence of a tuberculous cavern at the top of his right lung and signs of tuberculous softening in his left lung. His bronchial tubes were severely damaged. After seventeen days, the disease had greatly progressed and fever was continual: he was diagnosed with galloping pulmonary consumption and pronounced terminally ill.

The seminarian and his parents did a novena to Our Lady of Lourdes through the intercession of Thérèse, whose process of beatification was not yet open. Charles was wearing a sachet containing a lock of the young Carmelite's hair. During the first days of the novena, his condition got worse. On August 25, he coughed up blood violently. The analysis of the expectorated matter showed the presence of numerous Koch bacilli (tuberculosis bacilli). From August 27 to 31, he had a high fever, constantly between 102 and 104°F, along with vomiting and loss of appetite. While he was in a delirious state, the parish priest was called to administer him the last rites. Not willing to resign himself to this yet, Charles preferred to wait for the end of the novena. But on the last day, no change was noticed. This is when he remembered Thérèse's words: "I want to spend my heaven doing good on earth." Thinking there was some good to be done on his behalf since he was dying, he pressed his relic against his chest vigorously, and "[prayed] to the saint with such strength that, to tell the truth, the very efforts made with the aim of being healed should have resulted in [his] death."

Charles and his family began a second novena, this time asking Thérèse alone for the healing, and promising, if it was granted, to have its account published. Almost immediately, he felt a great change in his condition. The feeling of suffocation ceased, the fever disappeared, appetite and strength came back. The two physicians noticed that all the pulmonary lesions were healed and that the caverns had disappeared. His breathing still remained a little wheezy, but all symptoms soon disappeared.

Charles Anne during his illness

Charles wrote in 1907: "But while she was renewing my physical strength, Thérèse was also accomplishing in my soul a marvelous transformation. In one day, she had done the work of an entire life."

Charles Anne was able to be ordained a priest and became the chaplain of Lisieux's hospital for the poor. His miracle was acknowledged in Thérèse's beatification in 1923. While tuberculosis bacilli sometimes reappear after a few years, since at that point the healing dated back almost twenty years, there remained no doubt about it.

The first miracle acknowledged for the canonization was that of Sister Gabriella Trimusi of Parma, Italy, healed from tuberculous arthritis (white tumor) in her left knee and of spinal Pott's disease in 1923.

The second miracle was that of young Belgian Maria Pellemans, healed from intestinal tuberculosis, also in 1923.

Sister Gabriella Trimusi

Gabriella Trimusi was raised in the poor house operated by the Carmel of Parma, Italy, before she was taken in by a family. She began to work in a silk-spinning mill, where she suffered a lot from the humidity. She remained there until 1913, when she joined the Daughters of the Sacred Hearts of Jesus and Mary. She was 23 at the time. Hygiene in the convent was mediocre and many sisters died from tuberculosis. Gabriella Trimusi rapidly began to suffer from her left knee. In the end of February 1913, she first felt a faint pain that made her limp; her knee then assumed an abnormal round shape. Shortly afterwards, the pains became stabbing and prevented her from kneeling. The congregation's physician diagnosed chronic knee arthritis and prescribed iodine and poultices, which produced no effect, so that he decided to put her leg in a plaster cast for two months. After this, the knee still wasn't healed and the pains continued.

In 1918, no improvement was noticed. The leg was put in a cast again, to no avail, and then Gabriella began to feel pains in her spine as well as great weakness in her legs. The doctor prescribed hydrotherapy at Salsomaggiore near Parma, which only worsened her condition.

At this point the doctor suspected a form of tuberculosis. An x-ray examination on January 13, 1922 revealed "obvious signs of spondylitis between the twelfth dorsal vertebra and the first lumbar vertebra." Gabriella subsequently had to wear a plaster brace to immobilize the spine, once again with no result, and fever was soon added to the other symptoms.

In October 1922, she was hospitalized, in an attempt to treat the knee with x-rays, which also turned out to be ineffective. On December 16, 1922, after seventy-five days in the hospital, she came back to the convent and had to wear an iron back brace. The latter, lighter than the plaster brace, enabled the sick sister to get out of bed. The mother superior of the Daughters of the Sacred Hearts wrote: "But her condition was markedly worsening, she was suffering a lot and asked the good God for no other grace than to be able to hide her sufferings from her superiors, in order not to distress them. This condition lasted until the day she was healed."

From June 16 to 24, the whole community made a novena to Thérèse in order to ask, among other graces, for the healing of five sisters. On the last day of the novena, the closing ceremony of a solemn triduum celebrating Thérèse's recent beatification took place in the chapel of the Carmel of Parma. Sister Gabriella requested permission to attend it, "with the firm confidence that the dear saint would drop a few petals of her roses." Along with several sisters, she fervently prayed to the new Blessed. On exiting the church, Sister Gabriella felt pains in her spine, which she attributed to the efforts she had made coming on foot. Back in the convent, she told her mother superior that Thérèse had done nothing for her. The latter replied: "It's all right, pray and have confidence."

Right afterwards, Sister Gabriella went to the chapel for holy hour, and without realizing it, knelt on both knees without feeling any pain, which she had not been able to do for ten years. She explained: "Three times in a row, I felt violent pains in my spine, and at the same time, an irrepressible urge to take off my iron brace. Nonetheless I wanted to wait some more, but after dinner, the inner voice became stronger: 'Go, take off your brace, you are healed.' So I explained to the sisters this great urge I was feeling, and one of them told me: 'And after that? What if you fell down?' (for I couldn't remain standing one single instant without my armor). But I was feeling in myself the certainty that I was healed, and I replied: 'Well, in that case I guess the little saint is going to look foolish.' I went up to the dormitory and took off my brace.... I went downstairs in four leaps and there I was, with my brace in hand, among my companions, filling the air with my resounding cries of joy, my soul brimming with the most profound gratitude. I was perfectly healed."

In an instant the fever had disappeared; so had the spinal pains, and the swelling in the knee had completely gone down. This was rapidly confirmed by three x-rays, as the mother superior explained: "According to the x-rays, the disappearance of the disc between the two vertebrae and of the deep erosion of said spinal vertebra could be verified, as well as the healing of the tuberculous synovitis in the sick sister's left knee."

Maria Pellemans

In October 1919, Maria Pellemans, a Belgian aged 23, was afflicted with pulmonary tuberculosis, which very soon spread to the stomach and the intestines. Because of violent attacks of enteritis, she could hardly eat. In February 1920, her lungs became a little decongested, but the doctors told her that she had tuberculous ulceration of the other affected organs, and left her with no hope of healing. By July 1922, Maria was only able to swallow a little milk taken in very small and widely spaced mouthfuls. She regularly vomited blood and had attacks of abdominal pains causing her to faint.

LA PETITE
Ste Thérèse de l'Enfant Jésus
ET SES DEUX PRIVILÉGIÉES
dont la guérison miraculeuse fut adoptée
pour la canonisation.

(Reproduction interdite)   Avec autorisation du Carmel de Lisieux.

Sister Gabriella Trimusi and Maria Pellemans

Her confessor suggested she go on a pilgrimage to Lisieux on the occasion of the translation of Thérèse's relics from the cemetery to the Carmel, planned for March 26, in anticipation of her upcoming beatification. He told her: "You will see, little sister Thérèse will heal you!" She joined a group of pilgrims on March 20, though her condition was most alarming. On arriving in Lisieux, although Marie felt deep joy, her body was still suffering and the journey had only made things worse. She wrote: "After receiving Communion at the Carmel, I was seized with such excruciating pains that I thought I was going to die, and I lost consciousness. I was unconscious for half an hour, so they told me." After taking some rest, she wished to go to the cemetery to see Thérèse's grave. She felt faint once again and was unable to move for about twenty minutes.

In the Carmel's parlor, she asked Thérèse for healing "in order to be able to fulfill [her] lifetime dream: to be a Carmelite." She explained: "Until that day, the good God had kept me in indifference concerning my health, but from that moment on, it seemed to me I was pleasing Him by asking Him to heal me through the intercession of my beloved little sister Thérèse."

On March 22, she renewed her prayer to Thérèse when receiving Communion. Then, in spite of her fatigue, she requested permission to go to Therese's tomb again: "No sooner was I there than a very sweet and supernatural feeling filled me entirely.... Heavenly wellness was penetrating my soul and my body, I felt as if in another world, immersed in an ocean of peace.... After an hour, I believe, Father Barette, the rector of the basilica of the Sacred Heart in Brussels, and the spiritual director to our group of pilgrims, who took an interest in me, approached me. Giving me a beautiful rose picked in our surroundings, he told me it was time to leave the cemetery. I was filled with such extraordinary emotion that I thought to myself: 'Surely I am healed!' I was experiencing such calm, such inexpressible happiness!"

At that moment Maria was feeling no more pain, and her fellow pilgrims noticed the change. At lunchtime, she who had not eaten properly for three years devoured a meal at the hotel restaurant with a healthy appetite.

In the afternoon, she made several visits in a row without feeling any fatigue. Les Buissonnets, the Benedictine abbey, Saint-Pierre Cathedral: she visited all the places Thérèse had lived and came back in the evening full of energy, while others were exhausted. She even went back to the tomb to thank Thérèse. After attending the return of Thérèse's relics to the Carmel on March 26, the pilgrims went back to Belgium.

Having heard of this miraculous healing, her physician visited her as soon as she was back, and after examining her he exclaimed: "I don't understand, I find you completely changed, it can't be explained naturally, for the stomach and the intestines were incurable. Yes, if this transformation persists, we will have the right to call it a miracle."

Her good health indeed lasted. The physician concluded that "all the symptoms of tuberculous ulceration of the intestine [had] disappeared."

Maria Pellemans' father, very impressed by this miracle, wrote: "I must confess I was extremely impressed by this event, and it gave me deep confidence in Blessed Sister Thérèse forever." As for Maria, she joined the Carmel of Gand in Belgium one year after the miracle, under the name Sister Thérèse of the Child Jesus, and since her health allowed her to follow the austerities of the Rule, she took her vows there in October 1925.

THE HEALING OF SISTER CATHERINE CLARKE

In June 1908, Sister Catherine Clarke, a postulant in the novitiate of the London Bon Pasteur convent,[2] slipped on the stairs and injured her foot. In spite of rest and medication,

---

[2] Of the congregation of Our Lady of Charity of the Good Shepherd, founded by Saint John Eudes, dedicated to helping former prostitutes and women in difficulty.

the foot didn't heal; it remained swollen and discolored. After an x-ray at the Royal College Hospital, she had to wear a plaster splint for six weeks. After this time, no amelioration was observed and the pain was persisting. An attempt was then made to reduce the swelling by means of poultices, but to no avail, and an operation became necessary. Her parents wished her to leave the convent so they could nurse her at home.

Shortly after the accident, a medal of the Sacred Heart had been placed on Sister Catherine's foot, Lourdes water had been put on the dressings, a novena to the Sacred Heart had been made, and a number of saints had been invoked, "but heaven seemed to be deaf to all these requests." On October 30, with great confidence Sister Catherine started a novena to "the Little Flower," as she is called in Anglophone countries, and put inside her dressings a rose petal with which Thérèse had caressed her crucifix in the infirmary. She asked her to have mercy on her and to heal her in order to save her vocation.

On Thursday, November 3, Father Clarke, Sister Catherine's brother, came to the monastery to take her back to her family. She protested at first, but finally accepted, owing to the seriousness of her condition. When she went to bed around 9 p.m., she was feeling great pain in her foot, and beseeched Thérèse to heal her. Several times during the night, she woke up, repeating her prayer. Around 3 a.m., she woke up again, and realized her cell was filled with light. She related: "I didn't know what to think about this delightful brightness and I exclaimed: 'O my God! What is this?' I remained in this light for three-quarters of an hour, and couldn't fall asleep again, in spite of my efforts. I then felt the impression of someone removing the blankets from my bed and encouraging me to get up. I moved my foot, and how surprised I was to find the seven meters of bandages, which had been firmly bound and which I couldn't have dispensed with, completely removed. I looked at my foot: it was entirely healed. I got up, I walked, and feeling no more pain, I fell on my knees and exclaimed: 'O Little Flower of Jesus, what have you done for me this morning! I am healed!'"

At Mass time, when a sister came to take her to the chapel, she went down the stairs on her own, ran to her superior, and told her: "The Little Flower has healed me, Mother!" Father Thomas Nimmo Taylor said that "a kind of awe hung over the house with the feeling that God had been there." All the community, as well as the Mother Provincial and Father Clarke, could see that the foot was quite healed. Discoloration, swelling, marks of poultices and cautery—all had disappeared, and the foot had gone back to its natural shape.

SHE HEARD LOUD CRACKS IN HER LEG

On July 12, 1908, Antoinette Hébert was admitted to the hospital of Grandvilliers, Oise, to be treated for pleurisy. A few days later the infection spread to her leg, from the hip to the foot, which prevented her from walking without crutches. To this infirmity were added serious episodes of pains causing her to faint. No sedative could relieve her.

Antoinette was sent to Beauvais to be operated on by a surgeon of the Hôtel-Dieu,[3] but he didn't succeed in straightening her leg and declared it incurable. Over time, Antoinette's condition worsened. Three years later, she had lost 35 pounds, her hip was swollen, her knee ankylosed, her foot warped and crooked, her leg atrophied and getting shorter:

---

[3] A *hôtel-Dieu* was originally a poor hospital run by the Church. By the beginning of the 20th century, the Beauvais Hôtel-Dieu was already a hospital in the modern sense of the term—trans.

it was over 5 inches shorter than the other. By May 1921 her leg was inert, and the poor girl, faced with helpless doctors who left her to her fate without offering any solution, or any other treatment than morphine, was completely discouraged.

Moved with compassion, one of the nurses advised her to ask for healing through the intercession of Thérèse, and gave her an image as well as a relic from the curtain of the Carmel's infirmary bed. A novena was begun on May 14. For the first six days, nothing happened. On the seventh day, at 2 a.m., while (unusually for her) sound asleep, Antoinette heard a very gentle voice telling her: "Wake up!... Wake up!" Surprised, she thought she was dreaming and tried to go back to sleep. She again heard: "Wake up!... Wake up!..." So she slightly lifted her eyelids, and saw nothing unusual. A third time the mysterious voice said: "Wake up!"

This caused a frightened Antoinette to sit up straight in her bed and look all around. She didn't see anybody, but suddenly heard loud cracks in her leg, without feeling the least pain. She noticed with astonishment that her foot, which had been ankylosed and immobile, was beginning to move without difficulty, "as if set in motion by an invisible hand." All pain disappeared. She couldn't go back to sleep, and waited for the dawn. At 7 a.m., when a nun came to give her the usual morphine injection, Antoinette sent her away. She then decided to try getting out of bed. Much to her joy, she succeeded in making a few movements and understood she had not been dreaming. Not daring to walk on her own, she called her nurse and told her: "Sister, I have something to tell you..." "Quickly, tell me!" "Sister, look, I am leaning on my foot!" Filled with emotion, the nun stammered: "Walk!" Antoinette started to take a few confident steps, and suddenly began to jump with happiness. Very soon, everyone was shouting: "Antoinette can walk! . . . Antoinette is healed!" She was asked: "What happened to you?" to which she replied: "It was little sister Thérèse who healed me."

The healing was complete: the foot was straightened, the hip bones were realigned, the knee had regained flexibility, and the leg had grown longer. Within a few days, she also regained the weight she had lost. But the healing was not only physical. Antoinette bore witness to it: she also felt a profound change in her soul.

BURNED FINGER HEALED BEFORE THE SHRINE

In 1925, Doctor Aguerre had been a radiologist for about twenty years. Working without protection, he was suffering from radiodermatitis burns on his left hand, and one of his lesions, located near the nail of his left forefinger, had become an epitheliomatous ulcer (cancerous tumor). Five years of treatments had produced no results, and the burn, which healed from time to time thanks to the application of dressings, reopened very frequently, causing bleeding and piercing pains up to the shoulder. At that point, amputation of the third phalanx of the left forefinger was being considered in order to avoid the worsening of his condition, or even death.

At the end of March 1930, Doctor Aguerre went to Alençon, where he visited Thérèse's birth house, then to Lisieux, where he went to the Carmel's chapel in order to kneel before the relics and to thank Thérèse for favors granted. He took advantage of the opportunity to ask for new spiritual graces, "unwilling to bother her with material things concerning which [he] had put himself unconditionally in God's hands." But when his prayer came to an end, it occurred to him to touch the railing of the shrine's chapel with his injured finger, which had been particularly painful recently and had bled a lot. When he left the chapel, the pain subsided and the bleeding stopped. On the following day the wound was healed. When he wrote to the Carmel in August 1930, the wound had not once reopened, which had never happened over such a long period during the five years of the injury, in spite of treatments and dressings.

In his letter to the Carmel, he gave the following testimony: "I wanted to report it to you, so that you too could share our joy and would see how your holy little sister keeps her promise to let fall a real shower of roses in the form of extraordinary graces. There's no need to say how grateful I am to her, and that I lose no opportunity to tell everyone Saint Thérèse of the Child Jesus represents one of the greatest marvels the Lord has deigned to send us in these modern days, to show us His goodness and His infinite mercy, and to encourage us to turn towards Him and to talk to Him with the utmost confidence, in spite of our littleness and our poor human nature, sure as we are to find a divine recompense if we really place ourselves in His arms and completely abandon ourselves to Him."

HEALED FROM SNAKEBITE

In 1951, on the island of Pamanghat, on the Western coast of Borneo, a Franciscan congregation founded a boarding school. One day, while going to the marketplace, one of its pupils was bitten by a venomous snake. In an attempt to rescue her, she was given several injections, to no avail. Her body was gradually turning blue: she was dying, and was administered the last rites.

A nun went to the chapel and came back with a little statue of Saint Thérèse, which she put in the girl's arms. Immediately, her pulse could be felt again and she came back to life.

HEALED AFTER FALLING OFF A HORSE

In March 1973, N. fell off a horse. Her head hit the ground violently, causing a scalp wound which bled profusely. She lost consciousness. Two days later, as she was still in a coma, her condition deteriorated. Her right eye swelled for no apparent reason. She was transferred to the ophthalmology department. The surgeons decided to perform temporary tarsorrhaphy, stitching together the edges of the lower and upper eyelids. Following this intervention, N. gradually recovered, with longer and longer lucid intervals, but she still felt acute pain in her right eye.

One night, N. saw a radiant girl approaching her bed, all smiles. She was wearing a white dress and carrying something N. failed to make out, in an "apron" held up to her waist. The girl got closer to the bedside and leaned towards the patient. She showed her two or three rose petals, of a very pale, almost white or pink hue, which she picked up in her "apron" and then put on her eye. N. wrote: "Had she used them as a cleansing pad that she took back afterwards? At any rate she left no trace of them, but what I'm certain about is that from that moment on, I felt tremendous improvement and was no longer in pain." The apparition then said in a very gentle tone: "I am Thérèse of Lisieux. There you go. I must go. You know, I am in high demand presently, I have a lot to do . . ."—for it was 1973, the centenary of Thérèse's birth, when she was being particularly solicited throughout the entire world, with hundreds of ceremonies taking place in her honor. Thérèse then left, "neither turning around nor vanishing, but walking towards the wall, proceeding calmly and quite steadily." After her departure, N. felt immense peace.

On the following morning, the nurse came to clean the eye and was displeased, for it was full of dry blood. N. told her: "I'm no longer in pain, because...," without finishing her sentence. She then added: "Someone came to heal me last night." The nurse nodded without paying attention to what she was saying, probably thinking she was delirious. But as a matter of fact, her eye was healed.

Later that day, another nurse came and brought her a pile of letters written by her relatives. Since the intensive care unit didn't allow visitors, it was the only way for them to communicate. The first letter she opened was from her elder sister; it began: "I prayed a lot to Saint Thérèse..." N related: "Consequently I understood that if she had talked about another saint, I would have seen him or her. From that moment on, I have had profound faith in prayer."

N. had received a religious upbringing. Her mother had given her and her siblings lives of the saints in comic strips. The one about Thérèse had moved her less than the one about Joan of Arc. "For me," she wrote, "Saint Thérèse was the little Carmelite nun with a black veil and a brown dress, carrying in her arms the cross of Jesus and a bunch of roses, as statues depict her; nothing to do with this wonderful young woman!"

In spite of that religious upbringing, at the time of the accident N. was gradually drifting away from God because of her studies, which left her no time to go to church. She shared: "After my accident, I really had several revelations. First, that of the concrete benefit of prayer, and that Saint Thérèse actually was spending her heaven doing good on earth, according to her own words, which I heard of later on. But also that God doesn't abandon His own: that accident had come precisely at the right moment, when I was turning away from Him. Since that time I have been very fortunate."

While she remained slightly handicapped as a consequence of this accident, with balance problems, N. was able to lead a rich personal and professional life, in which prayer now had an important place. "I thank the Lord and His faithful Saint Thérèse for all that. And I even go as far as to thank them for this very positive 'shock' my accident was!"

TWO MOTHERS HEALED

In 1996, a mother had been hospitalized for ten months for cancer. Her husband was preparing their daughter for her death: "You know, Mom is very ill, she is going to die." Very soon, the doctors, thinking there was nothing left to do, decided to stop all treatments. Shortly afterwards, a woman in the same condition was brought to the same room. She had four very young children. The first woman made the following prayer: "Lord, take me and spare her life, my children are older, while hers are young. They still need their mother." Far away, her daughter, knowing nothing of this prayer, invoked Thérèse: "My Little Thérèse...," and then, thinking better of it, for she considered her a great saint: "My *Great* Thérèse, heal Mom so that she comes back..." On the following day, much to the doctors' shock, the two mothers had perfectly recovered!

HER HAND WAS HEALED AFTER TOUCHING THE RELIQUARY

In 2005, S. attempted suicide, which left her with a handicapped hand. As a consequence of a surgery, an edema had formed in the hand. Two of her fingers had remained deformed, insensitive, and without motor function. She was also suffering from arthritis and rheumatism. To make things worse, she couldn't afford physical therapy sessions.

In 2008, Thérèse's relics toured her area. On the occasion of a prayer vigil, she spent a long time praying before Thérèse's shrine and put her impaired hand on it. About to go away, she perceived a powerful smell of roses surrounding her, which persisted for a few minutes, even once she was outside. "It was heavenly," she wrote, "it smelled so good it felt a little bit like heaven." Following this phenomenon, she realized her hand was moving normally: the fingers had regained their motor function. "To me, it seemed extraordinary, I couldn't sleep all night, I was so happy!" she related.

The next day she went to the doctor. He confirmed her healing, which normally should have taken two years. The edema had resorbed, arthritis and rheumatism had disappeared. In an instant her hand was back to normal, which should have been impossible without surgery.

S. concluded: "I thank Saint Thérèse often for her intercession with God and for this somewhat miraculous healing. God didn't want me to remain with this handicap, and He didn't want me to die in August 2005. He will always remain in my heart, and so will Saint Thérèse, and I will eternally, forever, be grateful to them. Saint Thérèse has changed my life into a shower of roses."

Conversions

"**I** CAME HERE TO SAVE SOULS AND ABOVE ALL to pray for priests," Thérèse declared to the superior of the Carmel of Lisieux a few days before her profession.

Her desire to convert souls came to her after the "grace of [her] complete conversion" on Christmas 1886 when, at last out of childhood, she felt called to practice charity. She explained: "[Jesus] made me a fisher of souls, I felt a great desire to work for the conversion of sinners. . . . In a word, I felt charity enter into my heart, the need to forget myself in order to please others, and ever afterward I was happy!"[1]

One Sunday in July 1887, she received an apostolic grace in the cathedral of Lisieux while looking at a picture of Jesus crucified sticking out of her missal: "The cry of Jesus on the cross was also constantly resounding in my heart: 'I thirst!' These words were kindling in me an unknown and very strong ardor. . . . I wanted to quench my Beloved's thirst and I felt myself consumed with the thirst for souls. . . . I was not yet attracted by the souls of priests, but by those of great sinners; I had a burning desire to wrest them from eternal flames."[2]

At the time of Thérèse, the word "sinner" also referred to all unbelievers. To convert sinners made it possible to save their souls and enabled them to partake in eternal life.

The first sinner Thérèse desired to save was criminal Henri Pranzini, sentenced to death for triple murder. Thérèse ardently prayed for his conversion, and her "prayer was answered to the letter":[3] on his way to the scaffold, Pranzini seized the crucifix and kissed it three times. He would be

---

[1] *The Story of a Soul.*
[2] Idem.
[3] Idem.

her "first child." From this moment on, her "desire to save souls increased every day."[4]

On September 8, 1890, Thérèse wrote her profession note,[5] which she ended with these words: "Jesus, grant that I might save many souls, that there might not be a single one damned today, that all the souls in purgatory might be saved . . ."

The vocation of a Carmelite nun is indeed to save souls. Thérèse reminded Father Bellière[6] of the fact in one of her letters to him: "You know it—a Carmelite who wouldn't be

---

[4] Idem.

[5] It was customary for a Carmelite nun to write a few words of devotion in addition to the text of her solemn profession of vows—trans.

[6] Maurice Bellière (1874–1907), a White Father missionary in Nyasaland (present-day Malawi), one of Saint Thérèse's two spiritual brothers—trans.

an apostle would distance herself from the aim of her vocation and would no longer be a daughter to the Seraphic Saint Teresa, who wished to give a thousand lives to save a single soul."[7] These words of Saint Teresa of Ávila meant a lot to Thérèse, so much so that in 1896 she expressed the desire to be photographed holding a scroll on which they were written.

This is how, throughout her life as a Carmelite, Thérèse offered her sufferings and her sacrifices to save souls, encouraging her novices to do the same, her great desire being to "love Jesus and make him loved."

Thérèse didn't intend to dedicate only her earthly life to the salvation of souls, as she confided to Father Roulland:[8] "I would like to save souls and to forget myself for them; I would like to save some even after my death."[9]

The conversion graces described in this section show that some souls found the way to salvation through her posthumous intercession. Even better, among these saved souls, some evangelized others in turn. This echoes what Thérèse wrote to Céline: "Our mission as Carmelites is to mold Gospel workers who will save thousands of souls to which we will be mothers."[10]

These conversions were obtained in several ways: after reading *The Story of a Soul*, after a miraculous healing, after a novena, or through the use of an image or a relic. We encounter different types of conversions: a change of religion, the conversion of non-believers, or Catholics returning to God after getting into bad habits or no longer practicing their faith.

---

[7] Letter of October 21, 1896.
[8] Adolphe Roulland (1870–1934), a priest of the Paris Foreign Missions and a missionary in Su-Tchen, China, Thérèse's other spiritual brother—trans.
[9] Letter of March 19, 1897.
[10] Letter of August 15, 1892.

Saint Thérèse's writings moved a very large number of people, and even touched some of them to the point of inciting a conversion or reversion.

Conversion of Pastor Alexander James Grant

Alexander James Grant was born in 1854 in Scotland. A pastor of the United Free Church of Scotland in Lochranza on the Isle of Arran, in September 1900 he married Ethel Dalley, an Anglican twenty years his junior. She converted to Catholicism against her husband's advice on July 20, 1908, forcing him to resign his position as a pastor and to move to Edinburgh.

Now a fervent admirer of Thérèse, Ethel left in her husband's library an issue of *The Catholic Herald* containing a short biography of the "Little Flower" and announcing the upcoming release of the English translation of *The Story of a Soul*. Interested, the pastor carefully cut out the announcement and put it in his wallet, and afterwards kept asking his wife if the famous book had yet been released.

At Christmas 1909, Alexander, suffering from influenza, was confined to bed. He made the most of the situation by at last "avidly" reading Thérèse's autobiography, and was deeply affected by it. He would relate in his testimony at the ordinary process: "I owe my conversion to reading the life of Sister Thérèse.... I was of the opinion that I had come across the work of a genius, of a theologian, as well as of a first-rate poet. I can't convey adequately the extraordinary impression reading this life made on me. It made me feel like someone before whom the invisible world would suddenly open up."

Ethel Grant and Alexander James

He several times felt Thérèse's presence by his side, and had the impression of hearing her speaking to him and telling him: "This is how Catholic saints love Jesus; choose my Little Way." To which he replied: "Well then, I will try to follow it, if you help me." However the pastor was not ready yet to give up his Protestant faith. Once recovered, he gradually resumed his usual readings and distanced himself from Catholicism and from Thérèse.

In August 1910, Alexander once again felt Thérèse's presence. He recounted: "Another time, with nothing to warn me or prepare me for this visit, I felt the Servant of God by my side, and after the appeal of this presence had disappeared, I was left with these words, which seemed to be echoing in my mind: 'Can rationalism be true, and a life of such beauty and such sweetness be a lie?' I became convinced it was impossible, and that the faith that could generate such a life had to be a great reality."

The following month, he bought the complete life of Thérèse in French. He happened to make this purchase on the last day of a novena some friends were doing for him, unbeknownst to him. From this time on he started invoking Thérèse for help, and heard these words: "Why are you asking me to pray for you, while you ignore the Blessed Virgin?" Indeed, Marian devotion is inconceivable for a Scottish Presbyterian. This remark from Thérèse changed his view on the Virgin and he began to invoke her: "On the spot," he explained, "an extraordinary love filled my heart. Whither was she leading me? I didn't know then; but I was sometimes surprised by the feelings that possessed me and by the change that was taking place in my views regarding the Catholic faith."

For several months, he felt Thérèse's presence, prompting him "to practice generosity"; then, within the month preceding his abjuration, nothing, except "struggle, doubt and obscurity," and still a certain number of tenacious prejudices against Catholicism. The turning point for his conversion wasn't by means of supernatural interventions, but by real-life interactions with a nun in Edinburgh. The last hurdle the pastor had to overcome was to bring himself to believe in the Real Presence. To this end, he made a novena to Thérèse. During this novena, the nun who was instructing him took him with her to visit her convent's chapel, and this is how something clicked: "There, I somehow had the feeling of Our Lord's presence in the tabernacle, and on my way out I told the nun I previously mentioned, who was waiting for me: 'I now believe he is here. I felt it: something that wasn't there for me before, and now is.'" Alexander was ready.

After these months of inner struggle, on April 9, 1911, the date Thérèse had entered Carmel, he wrote to his ecclesiastical superiors to inform them that his convictions were no longer in alignment with the Presbyterian faith. He abjured on April 20, 1911 and was baptized on the same day in the Sacred Heart Church in Edinburgh, with the name François-Marie-Thérèse, a reference to Thérèse's baptism name.

Having thus lost his livelihood, the former pastor received material support from Thérèse: "On a Thursday of May, alone in my room in Edinburgh during the afternoon, I saw Sister Thérèse standing by my side and looking towards Glasgow; at the same time I had an inner feeling she was doing something for me in that city. My wife coming in presently, I told her: 'Thérèse is taking care of us right now.' On the following Thursday, an extraordinary and unexpected aid came from Glasgow. Since that day, I have had unwavering confidence in the little Carmelite of Lisieux and she continues to assist me in my spiritual and material needs."

Alexander James Grant gave his testimony in Lisieux shortly afterwards at the ordinary process, on August 8, 1911. On this occasion, the couple received the offer to come and settle in Alençon as caretakers of Thérèse's birth house on Saint-Blaise

Street. They moved in on June 3, 1912. Three years later, he testified again at the apostolic process, on May 31, 1915. He mentioned the reputation of sainthood of the Servant of God, as seen in his experience with the pilgrims. He passed away on July 19, 1917, aged 63, after uttering these words: "Little Thérèse, come and fetch me if it is God's will, and take me with you."

Thérèse brings a woman to realize her guilt and helps her make amends for it

Account by Mrs. X.:

S. (France)
July 11, 1917

I am reporting with deep gratefulness the touching grace Sister Thérèse of the Child Jesus favored me with in spite of my unworthiness.

At the beginning of my marriage, I lived with my husband at the house of his parents, who were managing a small business. But pushed by the inner demon of covetousness, I had taken on the sad habit of stealing money from the store's cash register, and little by little I thus stole a rather large sum of money.

I had no remorse until November 1915, when I bought the volume of Sister Thérèse of the Child Jesus's life. One day while I was reading it, a sweet smell came out of it and at the same time I felt deep compunction for my fault. Very soon, unable to resist any longer, I resolved to give back all I had amassed, but I wished to do it unbeknownst to all. So, knowing where my parents-in-law usually put their money, and making the most of a moment when I was alone at home, I went to their safe. However it was closed by means of a code I had no clue about, having never seen it being opened, and what's more, never in my life had I touched a safe. So in my extreme and insurmountable predicament, I called Sister Thérèse to my rescue. *And it happened that at the very moment, before I made any effort, the small but heavy door of the safe opened up before me!* Trembling with emotion, I left there the stolen sum of money, and that evening I had another remarkable sign, leading me to understand with great consolation that God was pleased with the act carried out through the influence of Sister Thérèse.

For the greater glory of this saint, I authorize the publication of this fact, and commend myself to her more than ever.

Mrs. X

Testimony of this lady's director:

Abbey of X.
July 17, 1917

Reverend Mother,

I hereby send you the account Mrs. X. was anxious would reach you through my hands. I assure you she's perfectly sincere; she has a right judgment, and since she has been acquainted with your little saint, she has found herself transformed to the extent of now being a daily communicant.

I must also tell you, Reverend Mother, that on reading this person's accounts, mysterious scents surrounded me, enough to convince me, if I still had doubts about it, of the truthfulness of the tale I am passing on.

Yours faithfully,

Rev. Fr. M. A.,
priest, Trappist monk

Conversion of a young sailor

Account by P. H.

Yokohama (Japan)
March, 27, 1924

Reverend Mother,

I don't really know how to express my gratitude to Blessed Thérèse of the Child Jesus; all that I can tell you is she converted me and helped me imitate the prodigal son in my repentance.

I was brought up in the Christian faith by my parents, who were very faithful to the laws of the Church; but I left my father's house at 14 to be a sailor, and there I only came across bad examples. Weak-minded as I am, I let myself be influenced, and I eventually forgot all my duties towards God; for five years, I even neglected to fulfill my Easter duty. Aged 20, as a navy conscript, I left for the Brest Arsenal, then for Lorient,[11] where I joined the Marine Battalion,[12] and it was thus that I boarded the cruiser *Jules Ferry*, heading to the Far East.

The ship's chaplain gave me a little pamphlet containing the summary of Sister Thérèse's life, but it didn't have much influence on me, though it reminded me of my faith. Later on, however, I read *The Story of a Soul*. Ah, Reverend Mother! You can't understand what it did to me after reading only a few pages. I immediately repented of having offended so good a God, according to what the Blessed teaches us. And the more I read, the more my heart was filled with bitterness; and I began to cry... Yes, Reverend Mother, I cried, and I asked the "Little Queen," as her father called her, to come

---

[11] Brest and Lorient, two port cities in Brittany, France. The Brest Arsenal is an important navy base—trans.

[12] The corps in question is the French battalion of *Fusiliers Marins,* literally "Marine Fusiliers," which still exists today—trans.

to my rescue and not to let me fall into hell, which would have opened up wide for me, had she not unpetalled on my route a rose of salvation.

I did the novena to "the Little Thérèse" to obtain the grace of turning my life around, and after these nine days, I went to confession. I now confide in my dear protector so as to always keep on the right track, and go to join her in heaven close to the good God.

I hear she'll soon be canonized; I assure you I'm delighted about it!

Please be sure, Reverend Mother, of my sincere repentance for my guilty past, and of my deep attachment to Sister Thérèse of the Child Jesus who saved me.

P. H.
Commissioned marine officer
Aboard the *Jules Ferry*

Oleg Tronko: an Eastern Orthodox turned Catholic

The Story of a Soul was translated into Russian only in 1955, after several unfinished attempts. But as early as the very beginning of the twentieth century, devotion to Saint Thérèse had been spread across Russia through the expatriate French Catholic communities, in particular through their teachers, as well as through Father Pie Eugène Joseph Neveu.[13]

The Story of a Soul was therefore discovered in French first; then in 1914 the *Vie Abrégée* (Abridged Life) was translated into Russian. In 1928 Bishop Michel d'Herbigny, main counselor of the Holy See for Russian matters, wrote a prayer to Saint Thérèse. Devotional images reproducing this text in different languages were widely distributed. Very soon, Saint

---

[13] Pie Eugène Joseph Neveu (1877–1946), an Assumptionist priest, later the apostolic administrator of Moscow—trans.

Thérèse was entrusted with protecting the Russian Pontifical Seminary (the Russicum in Rome), and was then named the patron saint of Catholics in Russia by Pope Pius XI.

In the late 1930's, a young Eastern Orthodox Russian named Oleg Tronko would be converted by Saint Thérèse. Born on July 7, 1918 in Kiev, right in the middle of the Russian Revolution, he emigrated to Bulgaria with his family when he was still a child. A true patriot, as a teenager he joined a national organization for Russia.

His family was Eastern Orthodox with the exception of his mother, a Catholic. She had enrolled her daughter Helen in the French boarding school run by the Daughters of Saint Joseph in Sofia. Oleg and his brothers, uncompromising in their Eastern Orthodox beliefs, were forbidden to visit their little sister so as not to have a bad influence on her. Furious at this interdiction, they threatened to go and make a scene outside the boarding school. In order to avoid this, Miss Zlatka, a young Catholic and a member of Pax Romana— an international organization dedicated to mutual assistance between university students and to promoting peace, created after World War I—offered to take them to see their sister. During this exchange, the brothers threatened little Helen that they would regard her no longer as a Russian if she became Catholic.

After this stormy meeting, the student confided to the young men that she had converted to Catholicism. The brothers Tronko consequently decided to bring her back to Eastern Orthodoxy, but the opposite happened to Oleg. Two days later, he went back to Miss Zlatka's lodging to ask for her help in his endeavor to learn the French language. A copy of *La Vie de Sainte Thérèse* (The Life of Saint Thérèse) lying on her desktop drew his attention. After agreeing to give her

Russian lessons in exchange for French lessons, Oleg came back every evening. The language lessons rapidly became religious debates. One day, Oleg asked permission to examine the portrait of Saint Thérèse used as the frontispiece of *The Story of a Soul* and contemplated it at length.

On Christmas day, he decided to draw a picture of Saint Thérèse. Wishing to make a success of his portrait, he invoked the saint, telling her: "Don't look away from me." At that very moment, he felt a deep change in himself, pushing him to follow Thérèse's way and to grow closer to her. He resolved to become a Catholic and a Carmelite friar. Showing his drawing to his friend, he told her: "I don't know what happened to me when I was drawing Saint Thérèse's portrait, but I want to be like her."

Miss Zlatka connected him with Bishop Kourteff, apostolic administrator in Bulgaria, who, struck by this supernatural conversion, accepted his abjuration two days after their meeting, on February 11, 1938. On the following day, Oleg received his first Holy Communion in the Catholic rite in the chapel of the Carmelite nuns of Sofia. From that day on, he attended Mass every day at the Carmel, though it was far from his house, and broke all his bad habits: tobacco, alcohol, etc. He had to leave the Eastern Orthodox high school he was attending and his father kicked him out, leaving him destitute, and soon familiar with hunger and poverty. Feeling compassion for him, the Carmelite nuns, poor themselves, offered him breakfast every day after Mass.

Having heard of his situation, Bishop Kourteff arranged for Oleg to be admitted to the Russicum. When he heard that the seminary was under the patronage of his saint protector, the young man exclaimed: "I am staying at her house!" Upon his arrival in Rome, he visited the superior of the Carmelite friars, who gave him a relic of Saint Thérèse, with which he would never part from then on.

A model seminarian, he put spiritual childhood into practice: his simplicity, humility, and obedience struck his confreres. Determined to follow Saint Thérèse's guidance faithfully, he read her autobiography in French in spite of the language barrier.

Like Thérèse, Oleg wished to aid in the salvation of sinners. One soul in particular was preoccupying him: that of his father, who was about to divorce his mother. On February 27, 1939, he sought advice from his spiritual director on the steps to take to convince his father to convert. The latter replied: "Implore the good God first, who alone can give him the light; don't discuss, don't reproach him, but write to him to remind him that life is short; put your father in front of death."

Unfortunately, the spiritual director didn't know how right he was. On the following morning, Oleg wasn't there for Mass. He was found unconscious in his bed, holding an eastern chaplet and wearing around his neck a locket of Saint Thérèse: he had died suddenly from a heart attack. Within a single year, he had displayed great fervor and followed Thérèse's way to the point of dying like her, hidden and unknown to all.

Drawn to Lisieux by Saint Thérèse

Account of R. P.:

October 23, 1997

Dear Carmelite sisters of Lisieux,

I am writing this letter to you to testify about Saint Thérèse. My story begins in November 1996. In spite of being baptized and confirmed, I had not been practicing my faith for several years and sometimes even made insulting remarks about the Church. So why did I for several nights feel a pressing call from Saint Thérèse, asking me to go to Lisieux? This call was so urgent, so strong (Saint Thérèse was preventing me from sleeping, I who insisted I had totally lost my faith, how ironic!), that I went to Lisieux.

I arrived in Lisieux in the morning just in time for a ceremony in the Carmel's chapel, during which the priest referred many times to the book *The Story of a Soul*. The excerpts read by the priest moved me so deeply that after leaving the chapel I immediately purchased the book, which I began to read during lunch. I detached myself from it with great difficulty to go on with my pilgrimage. I then visited Thérèse's house and eventually went to the basilica. I first went around it rapidly, but I had scarcely left it when I felt the need to go back. I had to go further, I had too many questions on my mind, I had to discuss them with a priest. Why was this happening to me, of all people? I am still grateful to this priest for listening to my words patiently, and I particularly remember one of his remarks. He told me "If Saint Thérèse has taken an interest in you, what is happening to you is not over, it's only the beginning!"

How right he was; it wasn't over. The following week, I feverishly read *The Story of a Soul*. Again came a call from Saint Thérèse, asking me to move on to the next stage, to ask a priest for the sacrament of reconciliation, but not just anywhere—in the church Our Lady of Victories in Paris. How impatiently I waited for that day! But what inner peace I felt after taking this step and receiving Communion during the Eucharistic celebration the priest had asked me to attend.

At that moment I felt, and it was very powerful, what the mercy and the love of Christ are for each of us. I was a lost sheep but he had not abandoned me, and through Thérèse he was showing me the right path again.

Then came a period I call my probation, during which I was left to myself. Of course I regularly attended Sunday Mass. But it is so easy to let oneself go and to slip back into one's old bad habits. It is so easy not to pray every day, to find "good" excuses for that. And yet prayer diligently performed gives one such joy, such a feeling of inner peace. But in order to understand that, I needed Saint Thérèse's help again. On my own, I was and still am too weak.

Since that summer, I believe I have understood, although I always lack courage. Prayer has become something very important to me; I need this moment of intimacy with the Lord; He gives me such a great amount of love during these moments. I like to pray to the Lord with Saint Thérèse and the Blessed Virgin.

P. R.

CONVERSIONS AFTER A HEALING

"But this disease wasn't there so that I would die, it rather was, like Lazarus's, so that God would be glorified."[14]

In many cases, people invoking Thérèse for healing are already believers. The healing obtained is therefore based on a preexisting faith, often a deep one. However, some of these miraculous healings are granted to non-believers or to their relatives so that the supernatural event they have witnessed might lead them to God.

---

[14] *The Story of a Soul.*

A young dying mother comes back to life, causing her live-in nurse to convert

Account by the parish priest

Saint-Nazaire (Loire-Inférieure)
September 29, 1915

A young lady in my parish, Mrs. L., was miraculously healed by Sister Thérèse of the Child Jesus this year on May 22.

She had just given birth to a little girl in very dangerous circumstances, and her condition gave cause for very serious concern. Three doctors had been called, and one of them, on leaving the house, told to the family in tears: "I must warn you that the case is extremely serious; summon your priest, it is high time." They rushed to the rectory; I was in possession of a relic of the angelic saint and I gave it to them. The live-in nurse, skeptical, nonetheless put it on the dying woman, who rallied in a prodigious and sudden way. Upon seeing this, the midwife exclaimed: "I didn't have faith, but now I am compelled to believe."

The next day, the happy mother welcomed me with a smile, and quite delighted, I baptized her little girl using the name Marie-Thérèse, in thanksgiving for the favor obtained.

This event touched me greatly and encourages me more than ever to have confidence in Sister Thérèse. I now place my parish under her protection.

Fr Crépel, priest of the parish of Saint-Gothard, in Saint-Nazaire

He came back to church after being healed

It happened in Belgium in 1970. J.'s life had been in danger for more than seven weeks: one of his lungs had suddenly collapsed and he had had to be transported to a clinic. A hole

63

had formed in the lung and the doctors were unable to reclose it. His sister-in-law gave him a relic of Thérèse and suggested he pray to her. His aunt, a nun, joined the prayer. Much to the doctors' surprise, the wound closed up. A surgery nonetheless remained necessary in order to put the lung back in place. J. dreaded this operation, but his condition kept getting better, and the surgery was soon off the agenda. Convinced of the intercession of Saint Thérèse, J. remained extremely grateful to her. He who had been spurning God after painful hardships decided to go to confession and to attend Mass again, which he had given up recently.

Healing and conversion in the crypt of the basilica

Account by JPG:

February 29, 1984

Here is the account of the grace I received from Saint Thérèse, evidence of her strength and of her love for mankind.

It must be noted that I wasn't a believer before Wednesday, April 25, 1980. It must also be noted that I had an ulcer in my stomach that caused me pain. On that very day, I was in Lisieux with a friend for business reasons. This friend, being a staunch believer, asked me around 6 p.m. to go up to the crypt, and knowing my views, was surprised I went with him.

In the crypt, on seeing my friend praying on his knees, I understood that something existed greater than I, and for the first time I asked God: "If You really exist, grant that Saint Thérèse would heal me once and for all, and then I will believe in You."

A few seconds later, an intense heat enveloped my head, and then went through my body down to my legs.

Since that day, I have not experienced any stomach pain, and on May 12, 1983 I received my first Holy Communion and I now attend Mass every Sunday.

Since this encounter with her whom I call my Little Sister, my faith has been immense and my joy unlimited to know that the Lord is by my side every day. I will never live long enough to thank the Little Sister for making me love Jesus.

JPG

***

GRÉGORY TURPIN, THE MISSIONARY OF SAINT THÉRÈSE

In 1994, as the centenary of Thérèse's death was approaching, her relics began a journey through France. From November 10 to 17, 1995, they travelled across the diocese of Pamiers, Ariège. During the whole week, talks were given on Thérèse and her spirituality. Ceremonies, activities, and prayer vigils were planned for children and young people.

At the time, Grégory Turpin, aged 15, had already begun a personal journey. He belonged to a youth group, where he was particularly involved in music. The arrival of Thérèse's relics enabled him to discover the young saint, whom he hadn't known. Through the various teachings and testimonies he heard throughout the week, he discovered a simple and accessible spirituality, based on confidence and abandonment. This first encounter with Thérèse touched him profoundly and marked the beginning of his spiritual life and of his faith.

During this week, Father Pierre Éliane, a Carmelite friar and a singer, gave several concerts. Grégory Turpin was struck by Thérèse's texts and by the way they were set to music. From this moment on, he used music to introduce a large number of people to the spirituality of the young Carmelite nun. In 2001, he collaborated with Sister Laetitia, from the

Grégory Turpin in concert

community of Le Verbe de Vie,[15] in setting Therese's poems to music. More recently, in 2013, it was he who encouraged Natasha St-Pier's to record her album *Thérèse, Vivre d'amour* ("Thérèse, To Live of Love"). Nearly 200,000 copies of this album, produced by French television channel TF1, were sold. He followed this in 2018 with the album *Thérèse de Lisieux, Aimer c'est tout donner* ("Thérèse of Lisieux, to love is to give everything"). In this way, Thérèse became known everywhere and touched a great number of people.

Since this first encounter in Ariège, Little Thérèse has never left him and has always remained present in his life.

CONVERSION OF THE INUIT

European missionaries arrived in Canada in December 1841 at the request of Bishop Bourget of Montreal. Six in number, they were Oblates of Mary Immaculate (O.M.I.),

---

[15] A French Catholic community, part of the Charismatic Renewal—trans.

a congregation founded in Aix-en-Provence by Saint Eugène Mazenod. Four years later, in 1845, Bishop Provencher, apostolic vicar of the archdiocese of Saint-Boniface (Manitoba), called on them to evangelize western and northern Canada. In 1895, Father Henri Grollier, O.M.I., reached the Arctic Circle and made contact for the first time with the Inuit, a people constantly on the move for hunting and fishing. For fifty years, the Oblates traveled the frozen steppes and occasionally came across the Inuit, but were unable to bring them to a true encounter with Christ. Only five or six baptisms were reported over this period.

On September 3, 1912, after spending twelve years among the indigenous Montagnais people in the area of Caribou Lake, Father Arsène Turquetil founded the first Inuit mission in Hudson Bay, after meeting them for the first time in 1906. This mission, located in Chesterfield Inlet, was placed under the protection of Notre-Dame de la Délivrande[16] (Our Lady of Deliverance), as Father Turquetil was from Normandy. Born in Reviers, Calvados,[17] on June 3, 1876, he had something else in common with Saint Thérèse: he had also been confirmed by Bishop Hugonin.

The first contacts with the Inuit were complicated and came down to trying to understand their language, in order to be able to communicate with them. When he at last succeeded in making himself understood, he was met with scorn and derision. The same year, two missionaries sent to Mackenzie were assassinated by the Inuit. Bishop Ovide Charlebois, apostolic vicar of Caribou Lake, gave one year to Father Turquetil to convert the Inuit, considered unconvertible, or else the mission would be closed.

---

[16] A Marian shrine near Caen, Normandy, not far from Lisieux—trans.
[17] Lisieux is located in the Calvados department as well—trans.

In 1916 an Inuit man he had never seen gave Father Turquetil two envelopes with his name on them. The sender has remained unknown to this day. The first envelope contained a very small book entitled *La Petite Fleur de Jésus* (The Little Flower of Jesus). It caught his attention, for Lisieux was his home diocese. Skimming through the book, he was delighted by the portrait of this young Carmelite nun of whom he had never heard, and discovered that she liked the snow, prayed for missionaries, and had promised to spend her heaven doing good on earth. The second envelope contained a paper folded in four, on which was written: "Dust taken from under the first casket of the Little Flower of Lisieux. She performs miracles with it."

Bishop Arsène Turquetil (on the right)

Father Turquetil immediately thought of invoking this "Little Flower" so that she might convert the Inuit. That very evening, he prayed to her with great fervor. The next day, he couldn't stop talking about her with Brother Girard, who was assisting him in the mission, and they agreed on a plan to convert the Inuit with the help of Thérèse.

In the evening, the Inuit coming back from a hunt joined the friars with the intention of getting warm. Father Turquetil sat down to play the harmonium, and the Inuit were standing behind him to observe the movement of his feet and hands on the instrument. Placing himself behind them, Brother Girard spread on their heads the dust from the cemetery, unbeknownst to them.

At first, nothing happened, but the following Sunday, the Inuit showed up for Mass instead of going hunting. Surprised, the priest thought they had come to mock him, but they assured him they were determined to have "their sins removed" and to change their life. He consequently explained to them that to do so they first had to get baptized, but also to receive catechism lessons. Father Turquetil prayed to Thérèse on the spot that they would accept the catechumenate, during which they could neither fish nor hunt, as it would imply leaving the mission for a long time. They accepted without hesitation, certain that God would not let them die of starvation.

Thus, for nine months, the Inuit attended daily Mass and attended a one-hour catechism course every evening. At the end of this time, Father Turquetil took great pleasure in baptizing four families on July 2, 1917, the feast of the Visitation of the Blessed Virgin. The "mission of the Eskimos" was saved.

On July 15, 1925, after a brief stay in France, Father Turquetil was appointed apostolic prefect of Hudson Bay, and placed his territory under the protection of Saint Thérèse in recognition of her help. He was consecrated bishop on February 23, 1932, in Notre-Dame Cathedral in Montreal.

Upon seeing what Saint Thérèse had done for the Chesterfield Inlet mission, Bishop Charlebois collected twelve signatures of Canadian bishops to petition the pope that Thérèse be proclaimed patron of the missions. The petition was sent to Rome in January 1926 and shown to Pius XI that March. The latter asked that all missionary bishops in the world join this petition. In March 1927, 232 signatures had been collected, along with enthusiastic letters.

On December 14, 1927, Pius XI declared Saint Thérèse of the Child Jesus "the patron saint, in a special way, of all missionaries, male and female, and also of all the missions in the whole world. She thus became their main patron, on par with Saint Francis Xavier, with all the rights and privileges that title involves."

Missions

"I WISH I COULD TRAVEL ACROSS THE ENTIRE earth, to preach your name and plant your glorious cross on infidel ground, but, O my Beloved, only one mission wouldn't be enough for me, I wish I could announce the Gospel at the same time in the five parts of the world and up to the most remote islands. I wish I could be a missionary, not only for a few years, but from the creation of the world and to the end of the ages."[1]

This prayer enables us to understand how intense Thérèse's missionary vocation was. In her day, many countries had never heard of Christ. Priests and religious brothers and sisters embarked by the hundreds en route to the other side of the world, often with no hope of returning, to reveal to these peoples the love of God. Louis and Zélie Martin had wished to have a missionary son; it turned out differently, as Thérèse explained in one of her letters to Father Roulland: "If they could have seen the future, they would have seen that their desire would be realized through me."[2]

Already at the time of her trip to Rome in 1887, Thérèse, aged 14, talked of this missionary zeal to her sister Céline: "I already have such a strong desire to be a missionary.... I want to be a Carmelite ... so as to suffer more in the monotony of an austere life, and this way, to save more souls."[3]

Once she had entered the Carmel, Thérèse practiced what is called the contemplative apostolate; for Carmelite nuns all have a missionary vocation, but their condition as enclosed nuns prevents them from being "active

[1] *The Story of a Soul.*
[2] Letter of May 9, 1897.
[3] In *My Sister Saint Therese*, by Sister Geneviève of the Holy Face.

missionaries."[4] Prayer and sacrifices are what makes them missionaries: they live "before God for all," according to the motto of Edith Stein.[5] In this way, they collaborate with missionaries in the field. Thérèse expressed this collaboration using the biblical episode in which Joshua combatted the enemy army while Moses was praying for him: when Moses lifted up his arms towards heaven, Joshua's army was victorious; when he lowered them, it was losing (cf. Ex 17:8–13). "Like Joshua," she wrote to Father Roulland, "you are combatting in the plain, while I am your little Moses, and my heart is unceasingly lifted up towards heaven to obtain victory. O my brother, how pitiable you would be if Jesus himself weren't supporting the arms of your Moses!"[6]

Thérèse very concretely experienced this mystery of the communion of saints. This is how at the end of her life, completely exhausted, she forced herself to walk and explained to her sister Mary: "Do you know what gives me strength? Well! I walk for a missionary. I consider how one of them yonder, far away, is perhaps exhausted in his apostolic journeying, and to lessen his fatigue I offer mine to the good God."[7] In the Carmel, Thérèse was entrusted with two missionary "brothers": Father Adolphe Roulland and Father Maurice Bellière, for whom she prayed and whom she encouraged with her letters.

Thérèse couldn't join the Carmel of Hanoi as she wished to, because of her poor health. She therefore had to be content to be a missionary in Lisieux by means of prayer and sacrifices. Yet she nonetheless became a missionary in the field

---

[4] Letter of June 23, 1896.
[5] Saint Teresa Benedicta of the Cross, born Edith Stein (1891–1942): a philosopher, a convert from Judaism, then a Carmelite nun and ultimately a martyr in the concentration camp of Auschwitz.
[6] Letter of November 1, 1896.
[7] *Last Conversations*.

after her death, as she had announced in her farewell letter to Father Roulland: "Be certain, my brother, that your little sister will keep her promises, and that her soul, delivered from its mortal body, will happily fly towards the far-away regions you are evangelizing."[8]

Thérèse was invoked very early in the missions. The first testimonies date back to 1909, only twelve years after her death. Bishop Thomas, a Dominican missionary made a bishop in Brazil, testified in 1933: "She loved [the missionaries] so much and, while she was on earth, already gave them so much of her good desires and sacrifices, that it was obvious a large share, a very large share, of her shower of celestial roses would be for them. And indeed, can we count on her favors, on her exceptional aid, we workers of the vast missionary field?"[9]

Thérèse assists the missions throughout the world. In 1929, Father Guilbaud, a missionary in China, wrote to the Carmelites of Lisieux that she was known "from one pole to the other." Her image was distributed to many families so as to introduce them to her. This is how numerous people requested her intercession in their trials. And there are many and varied challenges in the missions.

Thérèse helped missionaries themselves, for instance by healing them so that they could go evangelize, by assisting them in perilous situations in the field (accidents, shipwrecks, attacks, etc.), or by inspiring and preserving vocations. She also helped the missions' residents through healings, protection during floods, fires, epidemics, or famines. She removed the obstacles that prevented missionaries from evangelizing and populations from getting to know Christ better. She

---

[8] Letter of July 14, 1897.
[9] *Annales de Sainte Thérèse de Lisieux*, 1958, no 8, p. 22.

met basic needs and gave material and financial aid, but also intervened by granting symbolic graces that established lasting trust in the hearts of the newly baptized.

Thérèse, the Patron Saint of Missions, a painting by Sister Marie of the Holy Spirit, Carmelite of Lisieux (1892–1982), c. 1928

APPARITION OF THÉRÈSE IN SU-TCHUEN

Su-Tchuen, today called Sichuan, is a province located in southwestern China. Father Adolphe Roulland, one of Thérèse's two "brothers," was a missionary there from 1896 to 1909. Thérèse had hung the map of Su-Tchuen on the wall of the laundry where she worked in the Carmel. Shortly after Father Roulland's departure for China, she wrote to him: "Godspeed, Brother... distance can never separate our souls, death itself will make our union more intimate. If I soon go to heaven, I will ask Jesus permission to go and visit you in Su-Tchuen and we will continue our apostolate together."

Therefore one of the first interventions of Thérèse in the missions took place in Su-Tchuen, and was recounted to the Carmel of Lisieux by Father A. on July 20, 1909. He was especially wishing for the conversion of a particular woman. One night, during her sleep, this woman saw "a ravishing and mysterious being who was showing her the sky" without uttering a word. Questioned about her vision, she described the costume worn by this "being." Upon hearing it, the missionary was struck: her description matched the Carmelite habit, entirely unknown in Su-Tchuen. At the end of the interview, the priest showed the woman an image of Saint Thérèse, to which she exclaimed: "But this is it! This is definitely it! I recognize her!" These events subsequently persuaded the woman and her two children to attend catechism classes.

HEALING OF A DYING CHILD IN MADAGASCAR

On June 25, 1897, shortly before her death, Thérèse had told Mother Agnès, after reading in the *Annals of the Propagation of the Faith* the account of the apparition of a beautiful Lady clad in white by the side of a baptized child: "I too, later, will do the same with the little baptized children."

In October 1909, Thérèse's fame was beginning to reach beyond the borders of France. On the island of Madagascar, Mother Saint-Jean-Berchmans, the founder and superior of the Religious Sisters of Providence of Ambatolampy, handed out images of the young Carmelite nun to the inhabitants of the area.

In a village, a child was dying and his mother was mourning by his side. The missionary sister administered baptism to the child, then gave the mother the portrait of Thérèse, urging her to invoke her with faith.

On the following night, the family's home was filled with light. Thérèse appeared near the newly baptized child and placed on him a gleaming white tunic, the symbol of innocence. Before the astounded eyes of his mother, the child woke up and smilingly extended his arms towards Thérèse: he was healed on the spot.

A few days later, the Madagascan woman, carrying her healthy child in her arms, met the sister and told her: "The beautiful Lady you gave me healed my son during the night; I thought he was dead and was already mourning him.... And she arrived, carrying a white robe she put on him; and when he woke up, he was healed!"

HEALING OF A MISSIONARY WHO HAD NO CONFIDENCE IN THE INTERCESSION OF THÉRÈSE

Account of the Reverend Father T., apostolic missionary

Paris, 1912

Last year, at the beginning of June, I came back to France after twenty-six years on the Malacca peninsula. My health was deplorable; I was afflicted with acute and chronic dysentery.

For two and a half months, I followed with the utmost fastidiousness the prescriptions of one of the best doctors in Angers. Far from getting better, my health seemed on the contrary to grow worse. Inspired by the Blessed Virgin, on the feast of the Assumption, I went to the Carmel of Angers to ask the good nuns to kindly pray and have people pray for me. The mother prioress promised me to pray and have people pray for my intentions, and told me to begin a novena to Sister Thérèse of the Child Jesus. I admitted directly to this good mother that I had little confidence in the Servant of God. This confession somewhat scandalized her, I must say; nonetheless, urged by her, I began a novena.

In this novena, I prayed fervently, asking God, through the intercession of Sister Thérèse, to restore in me health of both body and heart. I was in a state of discouragement impossible to describe.

Once the novena was over, I went back to the Carmel more desperate than ever. Far from being better, my health was even worse. The mother prioress, after many encouragements, persuaded me to begin a second novena which left me in the same state. . . . "One more novena!" the mother told me for the third time. I obeyed without discussion and . . . once the third novena was over I was healed!

Thanks to Sister Thérèse of the Child Jesus! She is the reason I can go back to evangelizing my dear Chinese. Before leaving France, I was anxious to thank my benefactor by publishing what she had done for one who previously had no confidence in her. I hope the good little saint has forgiven me!

REWARDED OBEDIENCE

"Christ became obedient to the point of death, even death on a cross. Who after that would have the audacity not to obey?" we read in *The Imitation of Christ*,[10] which Thérèse knew by

---

[10] The quotation is not directly from *The Imitation of Christ*, but from the meditation added after Book 1, chapter 9, by Félicité de Lamennais, the 19th-century French translator whose edition Thérèse read.

heart. Already as a child, Thérèse was very obedient, at home as well as at the boarding school, according to the testimonies of her sisters in her process of beatification. Then, "in Carmel, her vow of obedience wasn't an empty promise," Mother Agnès of Jesus said. When the prioress had given a command once, "it was enough for her to make it an obligation unto death," Céline expanded, adding that Thérèse "judged people on their obedience to their superiors, and their works on their submission to authority." No doubt that the obedience of Brother J. C., whose account we hereafter reproduce, touched her. It is to be hoped, though, that if Thérèse had not taken the matter in hand so quickly, the superior would have had the common sense to send Brother J. C. to the doctor!

Saint Francis Xavier High School,
23, Nanzing Road, Shanghai, China,
December 6, 1913

Around mid-January, I felt in my knee a rather acute internal pain which gradually manifested itself externally by an incipient abscess. I could neither kneel nor walk with ease. I had had the same disease three years before and very quickly saw what was awaiting me: a surgery or a month of complete rest in the infirmary. I resigned myself to it.

Since the pain was getting worse, however, I went to see the dear provincial brother to tell him about my fears.

"What's that!" he exclaimed, "a surgery! A month in the infirmary! And who will teach your class? You know it, I have no one to replace you; ask Sister Thérèse for your healing."

"Very well," I said to myself, "now obedience is involved; Sister Thérèse will not resist."

That very evening, I began a novena and slipped a relic under the dressing, while repeating to the good little sister the command of the dear brother provincial.

When I awoke, pain and suppuration had considerably diminished, and they entirely disappeared that very evening.

I profusely thanked the little Queen and valiantly went on with my class.

But then, right in the middle of the holidays, the same pain and the same symptoms of abscess broke out in the other knee. It swelled a lot and the pain became very acute. This time I was determined to have recourse to the surgeon, but it meant abandoning my class again, for the holidays were drawing to a close. What was I to do? I again exposed my case to the brother provincial, who simply renewed the first command. I obeyed with the utmost confidence, and in the evening, before I went to bed, I put the relic on the sick part while recommending myself to my heavenly protector.

My confidence wasn't disappointed; upon awakening, all trace of swelling had disappeared; there remained only a dull pain, which also vanished the following day.

DROUGHT AVOIDED IN MONGOLIA

On October 15, 1918, Father Achilles de Lombaerde wrote to the Carmel of Lisieux in order to give thanks and to inform the Carmelites of Thérèse's assistance in Mongolia.

This missionary lived in the steppes of this country with a little group of Christian farmers. These people's living conditions depended on the crop; if it was good, they had enough to eat, if it wasn't, as in 1917, they had to go through a phase of food scarcity and eat roots and weeds, or else to emigrate to non-Christian environments.

The 1918 crop was promising well, but a big drought occurring in June seriously jeopardized it, worrying Father Lombaerde's faithful. They beseeched him to say Masses, to offer

79

public prayers and to expose the Blessed Sacrament in order to bring an end to this calamity. He began a novena to Thérèse to ask for her intercession, and celebrated a triduum to speed up her beatification. On the second day of the triduum, during Mass, the rain began to fall, reigniting hope in the hearts of all.

A month after this event, the drought reappeared. On August 5, Father Lombaerde made another novena to Thérèse. On the following day, abundant rain came to enrich the earth, thus allowing a fruitful harvest.

HEALING AND MATERIAL GRACE IN A MISSION OF ABYSSINIA

In February 1919, in the Catholic mission of Dire Dawa in Abyssinia (now Ethiopia), a little boy of two was suffering from a disease that generally killed in three or four days. His end being near, the village spent the night by his side. The following morning, Brother Diego Joseph, a Capuchin missionary, advised the mother to rub an iodine ointment on the child and gave her an image of Thérèse, encouraging her to have confidence in her.

After his departure, the woman threw the ointment in a corner of the house and put the image of Thérèse on her son. He immediately began to fidget in the arms of his mother. A man witnessing the scene told her: "Put him down; then we will see if he is healed." Once he was put on the floor, the child began to run and to play as before. Filled with wonder, the parents took him to the chapel to give thanks.

In the same mission, one of the most fervent Christians, who was devoted to Thérèse, entrusted to her the success of some important business concern. To make sure he would be answered, he promised to give the missionary the most beautiful calf of his flock. Shortly afterwards, he received a grace well beyond what he had asked for. When the time came for him to keep his word and give the calf, his wife advised him to replace the agreed-upon animal with another one of lesser value, which he did, without the missionary realizing the subterfuge. But as soon as the following day, the animal succumbed to an unknown disease. Having learned his lesson, the man came to the missionary, confessed his sin to him, and brought the animal he had promised first. In his letter to the Carmel, Brother Diego Joseph inferred from this that Thérèse "likes to find righteousness in the hearts of her protégés."

MIRACULOUS CATCH OF FISH IN CAMBODIA

In September 1920, the prioress and foundress of the Carmel of Phnom Penh, Cambodia, Sister Anne of Jesus, related to the Carmel of Lisieux that "our dear 'Little Thérèse' is well known in Cambodia; for that matter she seems to be taking an interest in this faraway land which she sometimes favors with her celestial roses."

The Carmel of Phnom Penh has a particular connection with that of Lisieux, for it was founded in August 1919 by the prioress of the Carmel of Saigon, founded itself by the Carmel of Lisieux. Several missionary Carmelites from Lisieux stayed there during the years 1920–1930. One of them, Sister Marie of the Child Jesus, explained to her sisters of Lisieux that the monastery was located "in a poor village of Vietnamese and Cambodian fishers" whom "the river isolates from everything."

Fishing was therefore one of the main resources of the village inhabitants, and more broadly of the whole country. In 1920, however, it had been very bad for five years, leaving the population destitute. The recent establishment of the Carmel in the area had rekindled hope in the hearts of this people, whose faith was fresh and vibrant. The fishers commended themselves to the prayers of the Carmelites before setting out for the "Great Lake." But after several months, the nuns' prayers remained unanswered, and the fishers' nets always resurfaced without any fishes.

Faced with their own powerlessness, the Carmelites decided to send Thérèse to the fishers' rescue; they gave them little bags containing dust from her grave and recommended that they tie them to their nets by way of bait. Sister Ann recalled: "And, dear Mother, isn't it a wonder? Lo and behold, fish suddenly converged in such quantity they were forced to put a good number of them back into the water! The witnesses and beneficiaries of the fact never tire of expressing their gratitude to the angelic Miracle Worker, and this gratitude has increased all the more because of several healings attributed to her intercession."

A ROSE BUSH BLOSSOMED AGAIN IN SOUTH AFRICA

Account by a missionary sister, shared by Bishop Simon, apostolic vicar of Orange River.

Pella, South Africa

March 4, 1921

We just received a touching favor from Sister Thérèse of the Child Jesus. Our young Christians have particular devotion to the Sacred Heart, and dedicate their most beautiful flowers to decorating its altar. They were dreaming of adorning it with roses, but sadly, our garden had none. We had only a withered rose bush that, for six years, had refused to blossom. Consequently I said to the children: "You should talk to Sister Thérèse of the Child Jesus, for she and roses are well acquainted!" A fervent novena began immediately. As soon as the seventh day, to general enthusiasm, we saw four buds appear on the sterile rose bush! They promptly blossomed into admirable roses of various colors, and for three weeks, flowers continued to bloom, more and more fresh and beautiful; their extremely thin petals were of such a delicate hue that I had never seen the likes of them. A curious detail: these roses were of a quite different variety from that provided before by that rose bush.

That bush, which had been wasting away, has from that day on been full of vigor; its branches bursting with sap are already two meters [6.5 feet] high and are intertwined around the niche of the Sacred Heart, for whom Thérèse made them blossom again.

You can imagine the joy of our neophytes. Their confidence in the little saint of Lisieux is now unlimited. A Mysterious coincidence: this favor was granted to them right when the request of the children of the South African region was being written, to ask for the prompt beatification of the one they want to adopt as their official protector.

Sister Frances Thérèse

A PAINTING OF THÉRÈSE RESCUES A CHINESE VILLAGE FROM A FLOOD

On August 8, 1924, a small Chinese village of 220 baptized faithful, attached to the mission of Father Hopsomer, was being threatened by flooding that had been going on for a month. In spite of a hastily built embankment, the water was seeping in, walls were collapsing, and houses were in danger of destruction. Moreover, the wind was blowing violently and the returning rain increased the risk of a breach opening in the dyke. The village was doomed, and its inhabitants were exhausted and hopeless.

Warned by his vicar, Father Hopsomer urged that the village be evacuated, but the inhabitants obstinately refused to give up their houses. This prompted the missionary to go there, taking with him a painting of Thérèse. On arriving at the dyke, he asked the bargemen to take him to the village by boat. When faced with their refusal on account of danger, he sent word to the inhabitants that they had to evacuate women and children, and suggested to those remaining to put the painting of Thérèse on the most endangered spot of the dyke. They retorted: "But Father, the water is going to damage it and carry it away," to which he replied: "No, the Blessed is powerful enough to protect her image as well as your Christian community."

The following morning, Father Hopsomer heard that, during the night, the water had suddenly decreased and continued to recede: the village was saved. He spent the feast of the Assumption there in thanksgiving. As for the villagers, they didn't want to part with the painting that had miraculously saved them.

PROTECTION AGAINST BANDITS IN CHINA

Father Kevin L. Murray, a Passionist, was responsible for the mission of Kienyang in Hunan, China. In 1924, this province was being terrorized by bandits, who gathered their forces close to the mission in order to attack it, and more specifically to lash out at three inhabitants: two rich merchants, but first and foremost the missionary. On October 21, however, the soldiers in charge of protecting the town left their post without cause, leaving the population at the mercy of the assailants.

Taking advantage of the opportunity, the latter headed for the mission's gate. Since it was closed, they ordered the inhabitants to open it. Upon Father Murray's refusal, they began to knock it down. One of the bandits succeeded in passing his gun through the door and shot towards the chapel.

The missionary immediately rushed to consume the hosts and hide the sacred vessels, then took refuge in the all-girls school after barricading the door, and hid under the beams of the roof. There he invoked Thérèse and promised her a novena of Masses if she came to his rescue and protected the mission. Barely fifteen minutes later, just when the door was about to yield, the soldiers who were responsible for protecting the town came back and put the hooligans to flight.

Touched to have been answered by Thérèse the first time he had had recourse to her, Father Murray testified: "The little saint sent us help, right when the situation was getting hopeless.... Since then, my confidence in her has been unlimited."

HEALING OF A BLIND MAN IN AFRICA

Account excerpted from the chronicles of the Missionary Sisters of Our Lady of Africa—May 1925.

Chilubi,
Bangweulu vicariate (Zambia)

I had in my mission, a missionary recently told us, a poor pagan man, who had been blind for eight years.

He lived in Kalumbila, eight hours away from Malole, and he often told me: "Father, I would really like to come more often so that I could pray and educate myself, but it's really difficult to find my way when I can't see." "Well," I told him, "pray to Blessed Sister Thérèse of the Child Jesus to come to your aid, to give you back your sight, and then you can do what you desire!"

The poor man left, thanking me, and went back home. Every day, he prayed to little sister Thérèse, and then one morning, he felt as it were a hand being placed on his eyes, while an inner voice was telling him to go and wash in the river nearby.

He told his wife what had just occurred; she laughed. It didn't matter—he got up, ran to the river, washed, and oh, what a wonder! His eyes opened up to light, he could see! He danced with joy.

The miraculously cured man immediately went on his way to the mission, bringing along the stick he had used such a long time to guide his steps, so as to leave it as an *ex-voto* in the chapel of the Blessed Virgin.

There was great joy among the Christians when news of the miracle spread. Everyone thanked God for the wonders He enjoys performing through the intercession of His amiable little saint.

Sister Thérèse once again did the work of an apostle, by helping a soul of good will eager to receive an education: as a matter of fact, our protagonist successfully went through his catechumenate, and many other pagans drawn to the truth were led to the Christian faith by the account of his healing.

THÉRÈSE IN JAIL

Father Joseph Guilbaud, an apostolic missionary in Tengchong, Yunnan, China, was granted a grace through the intercession of Thérèse in 1913. From that day on, he continued to correspond with the Carmel of Lisieux in order to give news from his district. In the following letter, from 1930, he told Mother Agnès of Jesus how he had put Saint Thérèse in jail…

Reverend Mother,

On September 19, one of my faithful of La Koo, having quarreled with a pagan, was sentenced to eighteen months in jail with his opponent. The people of La Koo like to quarrel and quibble, but it's not enough for them; they have to exchange blows. This is why the magistrate, wishing to give an example, sentenced the two brawlers to eighteen months of jail. Of course it was a heavy sentence. A few days after it was pronounced, I had the opportunity to see the magistrate and asked him to pardon the two offenders. He promised this to me, but days went by without the culprits being released. Relatives and friends of the convicted Christian beseeched me to intervene again with the magistrate. I approached him a second time. I again received the formal promise that, out of consideration for me, he was going to set the convicts free. This time I was hoping my approach would have a more favorable outcome, but contrary to my hope, the magistrate kept his convicts.

What was I to do? I began to pray and have people pray to Saint Thérèse of the Child Jesus. I thought that she at least would hear our prayers, but I must confess that she, who usually refuses me nothing, also turned a deaf ear. "The magistrate being stubborn," I said to myself, "is to be expected . . . but Saint Thérèse, what exactly is she waiting for?" It made no sense. Therefore, on a certain day, as I was kneeling before her image, I recommended my district to her, all my faithful, the conversion of the pagans; then I gave her an ultimatum to the effect of: "Dear little patron saint of the Tenchong district, I have been entreating you for days to deliver my convicted Christian, but you are doing nothing. I don't know why you don't answer my prayer. Still, this won't do: if in three days my Christian is not released, well, much to my regret I will be forced to put you in jail with him; we will see then if you listen to me."

I waited anxiously; three days went by, and Saint Thérèse still wasn't paying attention to my ultimatum. So, keeping my word, I gave the convict a medal of Saint Thérèse and apologized to the dear little saint, telling her it was in spite of my inclination, but I had to follow through with my threats; it was up to her to have the convict released, and it would be with him she would exit the jail. Well, three days later, the Christian was released!

He gratefully wears the medal of Saint Thérèse and I, Reverend Mother, while relating this to you, am quite ashamed: what are you going to think of me, who take the liberty to treat your dear little sister this way? Having the audacity to put the saintly little Carmelite in jail, isn't that brazen enough? In my own defense, I will say that desperate cases call for desperate measures. Moreover, you will see that Saint Thérèse can do everything, but she sometimes demands perseverance; she wants to test if our confidence in her power is sound.

More than ever I put all my hope in her; she is the one who is responsible for the good done in this district.

J. Guilbaud

Father Guilbaud passed on this hope and confidence in Saint Thérèse to his parishioners. He told Mother Agnès of Jesus of the Feast of Saint Thérèse in October 1932: "Yesterday, I celebrated Holy Mass with the greatest solemnity possible. I delivered the panegyric of your saintly little sister and, at certain moments, I felt my eyes getting misty; I had a lump in my throat. I could see the congregation was sharing my emotion. I was pleased to bring them to love her who is spending her heaven doing good on earth. I told the congregation to have unlimited confidence in her, that in heaven the good God always does her will because when she was on earth she always did the will of the Lord."

Once again, graces granted by Thérèse increased the zeal of their recipient: "I often request her to put in my heart her zeal for the salvation of souls."

In 1934, Father Martel, O.M.I., was accompanying the children of his boarding school on a trip through the swamps, woods, and rivers between James Bay and Hudson Bay in Canada. These children were about to meet their parents again after two years of absence.

The group was going down the Winisk River when an accident took place. The river was deep and very rapid. It was bordered by big trees, the branches of which went above the water. While the rowing boat was going down at high speed, one of the children seized a branch and capsized the skiff. All its occupants fell into the water, but none of the children could swim and the shore was far away. The children were struggling and were beginning to drown, and the boat containing the food supplies was drifting away. Finding themselves more than 120 miles away from any kind of civilization, the shipwrecked victims couldn't expect any human aid.

Father Martel presently began to shout in the language of his boarders: "Children, there is only one way out of this: pray to Saint Thérèse." He then shouted very loudly: "Saint Thérèse, save us!" The frightened children stumblingly repeated this invocation every time they came back up to the surface, coughing and spitting out water: "Saint Thérèse, save us!" During a few endless minutes, they kept crying out fearfully, while sinking into the water and clutching to one another so as not to drown.

Suddenly, the small group was directed towards the shore against the tide. It gradually came closer to it, and could eventually stand on firm ground with no one missing. Father Martel later related: "Following a common impulse of gratitude, we all fell on our knees! With our eyes lifted towards

Saint Thérèse, above in heaven, we sent her our thank you. 'Thanks to Saint Thérèse!' was repeated many times with tears in our eyes and sobs in our voices!"

Even the small boat was salvaged by an oblate friar, containing enough remaining flour to last till the end of the journey, as well as the portable Mass kit (chalice, ciborium, paten, cruets). The missionary commented: "Saint Thérèse preserved the necessary things for us! How good she is! How powerful she is!"

FIREFIGHTER THÉRÈSE

In the 1960s, in the mission of the Nativity to the people of the Chipewyan in Alberta, Canada, Brother Louis Crenne, O.M.I., and another brother left the mission's territory to set fire to their pastures to prepare them for cultivation. They had set to work when a violent wind suddenly directed the fire at full speed towards the edge where dry hay was lying. All day long, the two friars tried in vain to prevent the fire from reaching the spruce trees, with no water in the field. Since it was the eve of the Ascension, the two friars decided to go back to the mission and come back after the feast day with reinforcements. But before they went, the brother, who was wearing a little relic of Thérèse, decided to hang it on the branch of a tree.

The following day, during Mass, a storm and heavy rain pelted the area. When they came back to the spot of the fire, the two missionaries found the relic intact, while the branch had been blackened by fire. As for the large border of dry hay, it had begun to burn in places, but the fire had gone out. At the end of his testimony, Father Crenne exclaimed: "Without a miracle, it's inexplicable! Gracious Saint Thérèse has delivered us from much trouble! Thanks and gratitude."

* * *

In these days, there are fewer stories of this type, since the missions have changed. The years 1970–1980 saw a change in the understanding of mission: no longer about a few people leaving for the other side of the world to proclaim Christ, but about everyone becoming a "missionary-disciple," according to Pope Francis's phrase. In his catechesis of June 7, 2023 on evangelization in the school of Saint Thérèse, the pope stated that "the Church needs hearts like Thérèse's, hearts that draw people to love and bring them closer to God," and that a missionary "is one who does everything so that, through his witness, his prayer, his intercession, Jesus might be known." This is what Thérèse lived, and what she still teaches us today.

Children

WHEN SHE WAS A CHILD OF 10, THÉRÈSE HER-
self was the beneficiary of a miracle. In 1883, shortly
after her sister Pauline had entered Carmel, she fell dan-
gerously ill. Headaches, dizzy spells, hallucinations: Doctor
Notta judged that her case was grave and unheard of in
such a young child. The family was extremely worried. Louis
Martin had put in the room a statue of the Blessed Virgin
known today as "the Virgin of the Smile" and asked his
eldest daughter Marie to have a novena of Masses said at
Notre-Dame-des-Victoires in Paris. During this novena, on
Pentecost Sunday, May 13, 1883, Thérèse's condition worsened. Her sisters Marie, Léonie, and Céline turned to the
statue of the Virgin, praying to her fervently. Thérèse joined
their prayer, and was healed after seeing the Blessed Virgin
smile at her.

Let us have Thérèse relate the event herself: "Finding
no aid on earth, poor little Thérèse had also turned to her
Mother in heaven; she was praying to her with all her heart
to at last have mercy on her.... Suddenly the Blessed Virgin seemed beautiful to me, so beautiful that I had never
seen anything so beautiful; her face radiated unspeakable
goodness and tenderness, but what penetrated to the depths
of my soul was the 'ravishing smile of the Blessed Virgin.'
Presently my pains vanished, two big tears sprang from my
eyes and ran silently down my cheeks, but they were tears
of unmitigated joy.... 'Ah!' I thought, 'the Blessed Virgin
has smiled at me, how fortunate I am ...'"[1] Thérèse in her
turn has performed miracles for children after her death.

---

[1] *The Story of a Soul.*

A little afterwards, barely out of childhood and shortly before entering Carmel, Thérèse catechized two little girls: "Before leaving the world, the good God gave me the comfort to watch souls of children closely; being the youngest of the family, I had never had this joy." It allowed her to see that "these innocent souls ... resemble a soft piece of wax on which can be put the marks of virtues but also that of evil" and that they therefore have "to be well formed as soon as their minds awaken."[2]

But the souls of children are particularly dear to Thérèse for another reason: littleness and spiritual childhood are the foundation of her spirituality. Thérèse's "Little Way," indeed, invites us to have the same attitude towards God as that of a little child towards his parents. Thérèse copied this quotation from the Bible in the second part of *The Story of a Soul*: "Whoever is a little one, let him come to me" (Prv 9:4). This verse is one of the inspirations for the "Little Way." She wished to remain little so as to expect everything from the Lord. "My joy is to remain little / So that when I stumble on my way / I can pick myself up very quickly / And Jesus takes me by the hand ... "[3]

Her Little Way is based on confidence, abandonment, humility, simplicity, and love in all the little things of daily life. It supposes that one accepts one's littleness and one's poverty, being sure of God's mercy. "Jesus delights in showing me the only way that leads to this divine furnace; that way is the abandonment of the little child who fearlessly falls asleep in the arms of his Father.... Jesus doesn't ask for great actions, but only for abandonment and gratitude."[4]

---

[2] Idem.
[3] "My Joy" (poem).
[4] *The Story of a Soul.*

After her death, Thérèse became quickly known by adults through the *The Story of a Soul*, her *Vie Abrégée* (Abridged Life), and many other publications. But children weren't neglected. As a matter of fact, a life of Thérèse for children told by Father Jean Carbonel, S. J. (actually written by Sister Geneviève, Céline Martin, and corrected by Father Carbonel), illustrated by Charles Jouvenot, was published in 1923. Sister Isabelle of the Sacred Heart, a Carmelite of Lisieux, published in 1913 a small booklet entitled *Le Secret du Bonheur pour les "petits enfants"* (The secret of happiness for "little children"), encouraging children to practice the same virtues as Thérèse. Other works also saw the light of day, such as the booklet *Deux Mois et Neuf Jours de Preparation à ma Première Communion* (Two months and nine days of preparation for my first Holy Communion), modeled by Mother Agnès of Jesus after the preparation booklet she had made for Thérèse in 1884. More recently, comic strips recounting the life of Thérèse and her family have continued to enrich this collection of juvenile literature, so that very often children do not hesitate to turn to her when they need help.

In 1930 a biography of Thérèse entitled *Aux Petits Protégés de Sainte Thérèse de l'Enfant-Jésus* (To the Little Protégés of Saint Thérèse of the Child Jesus) was published. It followed the foundation one year before by Bishop Suhard of Bayeux and Lisieux of the Pious Union of the Little Protégés of Saint Thérèse of the Child Jesus. This association aimed to "place children and young people under the special protection of Saint Thérèse of the Child Jesus . . . to provide for them good moral and religious education, based on the imitation of their heavenly Patron." Children below the age of 12 could be enlisted for free by family members or godparents, and receive a certificate and a medal. This pious association still exists today as the Association of the Child Friends of Saint Thérèse of the Child Jesus. The first Sunday of each month the pilgrims' Mass at the Lisieux basilica is celebrated for the enrolled children.

Miracles related to children represent 23% of the accounts of graces received by the Carmel of Lisieux. They involve children of all ages, from infants to adolescents. Thérèse sometimes also intervenes well before birth for women having difficulties conceiving children or parents wishing to adopt. Most frequently, parents or grandparents are the ones asking for healing, protection, assistance for their children or grandchildren, but children themselves also have asked Thérèse for favors, either for themselves or for their relatives (the return of their father from war, for example). In the letters from children can be found innocent requests, expressed with simple words ("My Li'l Thérèse, heal me from my owie"); full of the confidence Thérèse recommends us to have towards God. Some children include with their request or their thanksgiving a little offering from their piggy bank, used, among other things, for the construction of the basilica.

THE OTHER "LITTLE QUEEN" OF LISIEUX

Little Reine[5] Fauquet, a four-and-a-half-year-old inhabitant of Lisieux, had been suffering from phlyctenular keratitis since January 11, 1906. It was an eye disease deemed incurable by physicians, which was gradually making her blind. Her eyelids were sealed together, her eyes were red and irritated, and her cornea was covered with spots. For sixteen months the little girl alternated between acute symptoms and remissions. She

---

[5] Reine is a French female first name, after Saint Reine of Alesia, but the name also means "queen." Therese was "the little queen," *la petite reine*, of her father—trans.

suffered a lot at night, couldn't distinguish objects put before her, and couldn't walk alone. She kept her eyes shut most of the time, or else wore sunglasses so as to suffer less from the light. Her parents gave her treatments that proved to be ineffective. They consulted three oculists, who asked them not to bring back the child, considering her eyesight effectively lost.

Moved by this situation, a sister of the Providence school in Lisieux, in charge of the class of the youngest pupils, advised the mother to take the child to Thérèse's grave and ask for her healing. She encouraged her to have all the more confidence in the young Carmelite nun because her daughter was named Reine, a moniker Louis Martin gave to his daughter. After hesitating for a while, Mrs. Fauquet decided to follow the sister's advice after reading the *Vie Abrégée* (Abridged Life) of Thérèse. So she took her daughter to the cemetery and picked from Thérèse's grave two little geranium leaves, which she respectfully placed in her home. She also asked the Carmel for a novena prayer, in which all the youngest pupils of the Providence school joined.

The following day, May 26, 1906, Mrs. Fauquet went to the 6:00 a.m. Mass, with the intention of attending every day of the novena. She offered a candle to the Blessed Virgin in honor of Thérèse—Thérèse not being a saint yet, it was not possible to directly light a candle to her.

In the meantime, at home, little Reine had a violent attack, stronger than the previous ones, and then suddenly became calm. She was gazing fixedly at something and smiling. In her testimony, Marie Fauquet, her elder sister, aged 9, related in her childish language: "While Mommy was at the six o'clock Mass to pray to Sister Thérèse of the Child Jesus for our little sister who was blind, I saw her open her eyes suddenly, staring beside the bed. She was laughing, was stretching her little arm out of the bed, was moving it as if to play. I thought she was being healed, that she was seeing the objects of the house, but nonetheless it seemed odd to me. It lasted quite a long time, and then Reine fell asleep. I asked her afterwards what she had been looking at so much and why she had laughed. She answered that she had laughed at Little Thérèse near her bed and had taken her by the hand, that she was beautiful, that she had a veil on and that it was all lit up around her head."

Back home, after hearing her daughter had had stronger symptoms than usual, Mrs. Fauquet told her: "Put on your glasses, since they relieve you," to which the little girl replied joyfully: "Mommy, I don't need them anymore, *I see as well as you do now*." So the mother put Reine closer to the window to inspect her eyes, then called her husband and told him: "Look at your daughter! You ridiculed my confidence, well, look at her eyes! She is healed!"

Reine Fauquet

As a matter of fact the eyes, now wide open, were no longer red, no longer inflamed, no longer spotted, no longer purulent, and the child could see distinctly what surrounded her. She was declared completely healed by the doctor, and no relapse occurred afterwards. A dozen witnesses, among them three religious sisters of the Providence of Lisieux, the family's landlady, and Lisieux shopkeepers, confirmed this miraculous healing.

Some time later, the Lisieux Carmelites received Reine and her parents in the parlor. They questioned her about Thérèse's apparition. When they asked her: "What was she wearing, little Reine?" the little girl replied: "The same as you!"

ÉDITH PIAF: "SHE HAD CAUGHT ME, AND FOR LIFE"[6]

The most famous "kid"[7] healed by Thérèse is Édith Gassion, better known as Édith Piaf. Born in Paris on December 19, 1915, during World War I, she was abandoned by her mother at two months and entrusted to her maternal grandmother. The latter, an alcoholic artist, took poor care of the child, who became sickly and suffered from poor hygiene. Back from the war, her father decided to send her to Normandy to the home of her paternal grandmother, Louise Gassion, who ran a brothel in Bernay, in the department of Eure. Édith arrived there in June 1917. Aged 18 months at the time, the little girl was covered with scabs from head to foot. The doctor diagnosed severe malnutrition, bronchitis, and impetigo. Her eyes were watery and glued shut. Within a

---

[6] Jacqueline Cartier and Hugues Vassal, *Édith et Thérèse. La Sainte et la Pécheresse* (Edith and Thérèse: The Saint and the Sinner) (Paris, Éditions Anne Carrière, 1999), p. 116. All quotations of this section are from this book.

[7] *La Môme Piaf* (Kid Sparrow, or Little Sparrow) was Édith's nickname, and she ended up adopting Édith Piaf as her stage name—trans.

few weeks, thanks to the doctor's treatment, she was healed from her bronchitis and regained strength.

Around 1919, the girls of the brothel realized that Édith kept banging into everything and avoided the light. The schoolmistress also observed that she had poor sight. The doctor referred her to Doctor Degrenne, an ophthalmologist in Lisieux, who diagnosed double phlyctenular keratitis, and thought she had very little chance of recovery.

The diagnosis reminded Louise Gassion of the miraculous healing by Thérèse of little Reine Fauquet, which had been much talked about in the area. Like many people in Normandy, Mrs. Gassion had an image of Thérèse in her home, prominently displayed on her chest of drawers. She thought to herself that since Thérèse had healed little Reine ten years before, she could also heal her granddaughter, of about the same age and suffering from the same illness. On leaving the small room, she immediately took Édith to Saint-Pierre Basilica to pray.

Back in Bernay, she and her "daughters" treated her according to the doctor's prescription: an ophthalmic ointment applied daily to the eyes under a dressing maintained by a black blindfold screening them from the light.

The whole household was praying for her healing: "And prayers, since we are lucky enough to be believers. It's a trial to undergo. Her recovering also depends on us," Louise Gassion wrote. But every time the bandage was taken off in order to change the dressing, the little one still saw nothing. The doctor even suggested that they begin to teach her Braille.

But the grandmother had great confidence in Saint Thérèse. Thinking that the daily prayers of the whole household were not enough to obtain Édith's healing, she decided to close her house for a whole day to make a pilgrimage to Thérèse's grave. On Friday, August 19, 2021, four days after Thérèse had been declared Venerable by Pope Benedict XV, Louise Gassion, her five "boarders," and Édith arrived in Lisieux by train. The girls had made an effort to dress as modestly as possible: a hat, no makeup, no low-cut neckline or slit skirt, all clad in black right in the middle of the summer.

The first step of this pilgrimage was a Mass at Saint-Pierre Cathedral. Édith would later relate: "I fell asleep! When Granny shook me to get going, the Mass was over! What a shame! I had not kept my appointment with the little sister Thérèse who was to heal me. But she was not angry with me.... When later on I read *The Story of a Soul*, I was pretty glad: she too used to fall asleep during silent prayer!"

After picnicking, they went to the cemetery. Louise Gassion bought roses for each of her girls and for Édith. The little one weaved in and out between the pilgrims to go and put her rose on Thérèse's grave. Her grandmother collected a handful of dust in a bag and made the sign of the cross, while the girls were unpetalling their roses. Asked by Rose, one of her "little mothers" of the brothel, what she had told Thérèse, Édith replied: "I told her: 'Give me back my eyes, I can't wait to see you.'" Worried that she had not said a real prayer, she was quickly reassured by Rose: "No, it's all right. The little sister understands even the words we don't say." No miracle happened at the grave. The whole party headed to the train station to go back to Bernay, not knowing what to think or hope.

Over the following days Édith wore the little bag containing dust from the grave. At the same time, Doctor Degrenne's ointment was still being applied to her eyes. But she remained blind. Little by little, the grandmother was overcome with resignation, although she asked Thérèse one more time for the healing of Édith on August 25, Saint Louis's day, her son's and her own name day.

On the morning of August 25 Édith was not feeling well. She had a fever all day. Suddenly, around 7 p.m., she went down to the kitchen, holding her blindfold in her hand: she could see. The whole household was astounded. Édith ran to the living room towards the player-piano, which she had heard and touched, but never seen. Very soon, the doctor was fetched, and could only acknowledge the healing.

As soon as the next day, the whole household went back to Lisieux to thank Thérèse. The girls were no longer wearing black dresses, but bright colors and flowered hats.

After a call on Doctor Degrenne, they attended Mass at the cathedral. Édith was captivated by the sight of the priest elevating the host. She was also delighted by the Latin chant. Not understanding the lyrics, she began to sing her own made-up lines to the tune she was hearing: "Thank you, Little Thérèse! Thank you for your mercy! You're the reason I can see! And I'd like to see you also, before to paradise I go!" The trip ended with a visit to the cemetery, where Édith unpetalled roses on Thérèse's grave.

After her return, she went back to school and asked Thérèse to help her catch up with her schoolwork. As a matter of fact she did rather well. But it was now looked unfavorably upon that the little girl, who at that point could see very well, should live in a brothel. She therefore had to go back to her father. Before her departure, her grandmother put a medal of Thérèse around her neck, telling her not to forget that she would always protect her.

Two years later, Édith was giving performances with her father, he as an acrobat, she as a singer. One day, when she had a cold and a fever, she was advised not to go and sing. Refusing to obey, she prayed to Thérèse and made the sign of the cross before going on stage: "She sang as if the fever had never existed." She afterwards always kept the habit of saying a prayer before appearing on stage.

In June 1925, after she had been on the road with her father for three years, she decided to run away to see her grandmother again in Bernay. She asked her to take her to Lisieux to see Thérèse, who had been canonized in the meantime. This time, she didn't visit her at the grave but at the Carmel's chapel, where Thérèse now rested in a shrine.

All her life long Édith Piaf retained a particular devotion to Saint Thérèse: her portrait was on her nightstand and in her dressing room. She returned to Lisieux many times, accompanied by friends or lovers. As an adult, she read *The Story of a Soul*. Much earlier, she had read *Histoire de Sœur Thérèse de l'Enfant-Jésus pour les enfants* (The story of Sister Thérèse of the Child Jesus for children). This book made her feel close to the Carmelite nun, for in it she discovered that, just like her, Thérèse had lost her mother, that she had a surrogate "little mother," and that her father was named Louis. But she was even closer to Thérèse than she ever realized, for they were distant cousins on the fathers' side, sharing an ancestor in Louis Bohard, a native of Athis-de-l'Orne[8] in the seventeenth century.

"LITTLE FLOWER, BRING US BACK OUR BIRD!"

An incident at the boarding school of the convent of Saint Mary's in Standishgate, Wigan (England), reveals the power of children's prayer, even for as naive a request as the return of an animal.

The incident took place in November 1912. The youngest pupils of the boarding school had a canary in their classroom. During a momentary lapse of attention, it flew off to the garden, and in spite of the efforts of the gardener, the workers, and all the children, nobody was able to get it back. The men warned the sister in charge of the class that it was useless to hope for the bird's return, much to the little girls' dismay.

So the children asked their teacher to go to the park again while they would ask Thérèse to make their bird come back. The sister agreed, took the empty cage, and went back to the garden. The little girls immediately began to pray in their childish language: "Little Flower, bring us back our bird!" The innocence and fervor of this request moved the young woman in charge of looking after the class; at the same time she was afraid the pupils would be disappointed if the teacher came back with an empty cage.

No doubt this confident prayer also touched the Little Thérèse in heaven since, after being absent for fifteen minutes, the teacher reappeared in the classroom with the canary! After waiting for some time in the garden, the bird eventually came to land on the cage, then entered it through the little door.

---

[8] A town not far from Alençon, Thérèse's birthplace in the department of Orne, Normandy—trans.

THÉRÈSE DESCENDS FROM HEAVEN AND GIVES HER MYSTERIOUS FLOWERS

On January 24, 1913, in Ireland, Mary Mac Nelis gave birth to a little girl who was to be baptized two days later under the names Marie-Françoise-Thérèse—Thérèse's three names. Shortly after the delivery, the mother was dying. However, a novena had been started for her in the Carmel of Lisieux on January 20, and a portrait of Thérèse was hung above her bed. The young mother's relatives suggested to her daughter Kathleen, aged 4, to ask the Little Flower for the healing of her mother, and to promise her to offer her First Holy Communion in her honor.

The next day, the little girl brought to her still very weak mother six white flowers of outstanding beauty, little snowdrops. They were put in a vase on a small altar, without anybody attaching importance to it. A few hours later, an "exquisite smell" was emanating from those usually odorless flowers. The mother then asked the child where she had gotten them. The little girl replied: "A nun flew to me with them and said that mom would get better, and then she flew off." From this moment, her mother's condition kept getting better, and the smell lingered several more days.

ARTHUR POTOT: A MIRACLE ALMOST CITED IN THE BEATIFICATION

In 1915, young Arthur Potot, aged eight and a half, lived in Boulogne-sur-Mer in a poor family. He had been suffering from age 5 from a tumor in his cheek with decay of the lower jawbone. This tumor was causing numerous abscesses on his neck and on his cheek, which was so swollen it came down to his shoulder. A piece of jawbone was cutting his lower lip. He had been wearing a bandage around his head for three and a half years. Because of this frightening physical appearance, he was nicknamed "Rhinoceros."

The parents, who were very poor, couldn't afford to get their son proper treatment. They took him to the Red Cross or to the pharmacy, with no regular medical follow-up. The doctors recommended the ablation of the cheek but asserted that he wouldn't heal, for the jawbone decay was irreversible. The only treatment given to the child consisted in cleaning his wounds every day. He lived on bread dipped in milk, introduced into the mouth with difficulty. Little by little, the pains increased and the cheek swelled more and more, forcing Arthur to stay in bed most of the time, awaiting death.

In April, Arthur's mother took him to Miss Constance Cardon, a sixty-year-old philanthropist who assisted and educated the poor of Boulogne-sur-Mer. She asked Miss Cardon to have him make his first Holy Communion before his imminent death. The young boy consequently joined a catechism group consisting in twelve children aged 12 to 16, taken from the streets.

In July, Miss Cardon asked the children to do a novena to Thérèse to ask that their comrade could make his first Holy Communion with them, sure of the power of the children's prayer, faith, and confidence: "We therefore began this novena with much fervor; I never saw those unfortunate children—who come to God with a simple and confident heart, and as a result obtain choice graces from the divine Master—pray with so much faith." On the ninth day of the novena, no change was observed, but the children remained confident and kept praying to Saint Thérèse.

It was finally decided to have Arthur make his first Holy Communion alone, giving him only a small piece of the host.

The date was set for July 11. However, the day before, at 11 a.m. Arthur arrived at the catechism class with no bandage at all. He had no more abscesses, no more suppuration, no bone protruding through his lip, and no more wound. Delighted to witness this miraculous healing, the children and Miss Cardon fell on their knees and sang the *Magnificat* together, full of gratitude towards Little Thérèse.

When Miss Cardon asked him where the bone cutting his lip was, Arthur explained: "Yesterday evening, I was asleep, my elder sister removed it from me; I didn't wake up, for she didn't hurt me. It's Sister Thérèse who told her to do it." In her testimony on May 15, 1916, Miss Cardon gave details: "The bone of our little miracle-recipient was removed by his 23-year-old sister. On the evening of July 9, the child fell deeply asleep; his mother and his sister were beside him, gazing with sadness and compassion at this poor face disfigured by the five purulent abscesses, the swelling of the cheek, and the bone that was protruding from his mouth. Suddenly, Arthur's sister felt urged by an irrepressible desire and an inner voice to remove the bone. The mother was opposed to it, afraid of making the child suffer, but her daughter could not resist the supernatural impulse, and while her mother was hurriedly leaving, she came close to her brother and gently pulled the bone, which in an instant disintegrated, and fell into her hand. It was four inches long and one inch wide. All night long the girl couldn't sleep out of emotion."

After singing the *Magnificat*, Arthur, who could now talk, sing, and eat normally, easily swallowed a slice of bread and butter offered by Miss Cardon. Too moved to teach catechism, she sent the children home. Full of enthusiasm, the young boys took Arthur's hand and announced to the whole neighborhood the miraculous healing of their friend: "We have performed a miracle! Come and see young Potot. He's no longer ill! He's healed!" Arthur in turn began to shout: "I'm no longer in pain; Saint Thérèse healed me!" Very soon the whole district joined them in thanking Thérèse, witnessing the obviously miraculous healing of the boy.

On July 10, Arthur went on an afternoon of retreat with his comrades to prepare for their first Holy Communion. On the following day, in the presence of one-hundred fifty poor people gathered in the chapel of Saint-Michel Parish, he received Communion first, with no difficulty: his healing was complete.

Sixty people signed the testimony sent to Monsignor de Teil, vice-postulator of the cause for Thérèse's beatification. The miracle was studied, but unfortunately, since the child had been treated in a pharmacy and not a hospital, the instantaneousness of the miracle could not be proved because there had been no regular follow-up.

In a letter from Sister Geneviève, we read that the pope himself was informed of this miracle: "We just met Monsignor de Teil, who is back from Rome. He had only good news to share with us. As early as the second day after he had arrived in the Eternal City, he saw the pope in a very long private audience. No sooner had the Holy Father caught sight of him than he asked him: 'Well, where are we with the cause of Sister Thérèse?'; then he asked if she still performed miracles. Monsignor de Teil related to His Holiness a few of the most recent ones, among others the miracle of young Potot from Boulogne, and Benedict XV promptly replied: 'This is a true miracle.'"[9]

---

[9] Letter of Sister Geneviève to Sister Françoise-Thérèse, July 8, 1917.

THE STORY OF A SOUL SLOWS A CAR DOWN AND KEEPS A CHILD FROM BEING RUN OVER

In July 1916, a Mrs. Borda wrote to the Carmel to inform the sisters that her son had escaped a serious accident thanks to Thérèse. He was going to the house of a friend to leave there *The Story of a Soul*, carefully wrapped. On exiting the streetcar, he was knocked over by a car at full speed. Thrown under the car, he got up through "a powerful strength" and pulled himself out. He saw that the book, placed against one of the car's wheels, had served as a break, preventing it from crushing him entirely. The child got by with only a few minor bruises, while his clothes were in shreds.

THÉRÈSE COMES DOWN FROM HER PAINTING AND GOES UP AGAIN

On January 7, 1921, young Juliet Sompayrac, aged three and a half, was afflicted with headache on the way home from school. The doctor, fetched immediately, prescribed a bromine ointment, but the condition of the child did not improve: her left eye was very swollen; the joints of her limbs and of her backbone were affected. He diagnosed her with meningitis. Ice was applied on her head and several treatments were tried, but the little girl got worse and worse.

On January 11, her mother told her husband: "Let us write to the Carmel of Sister Thérèse of the Child Jesus; I am certain she will obtain Juliet's healing, as she has already been so good to us." She therefore asked the Carmel of Lisieux for prayers. A painting of Thérèse was put in front of the sick girl's bed. The next day, the doctor thought there was nothing more to be done, but nonetheless suggested doing a lumbar puncture. Seeing his lack of conviction, Mrs. Sompayrac refused, instead leaving the situation to Thérèse.

The little girl was extremely sick and was crying out night and day. Suddenly, on January 13, she sat on her bed and said to her grandmother: "The little Jesus of Sister Thérèse will heal me tomorrow." The whole family was astounded, since from the beginning of her disease she had not uttered a single word. The following night was horrendous. The child was seized with grave convulsions, frightening those present, so much so that her mother couldn't stand the sight of the sad scene.

On January 14, about 4 p.m., the family was gathered around Juliet's bed, waiting for her final breath, when she suddenly sat up straight again on her own and said with a smile: "Mama, Grandma, Sister Thérèse has healed me." When her father came home from work in the evening, she repeated the same thing to him. When he asked her who had told her that, she replied by showing him the painting of Thérèse: "Why, it was she, obviously!" When the doctor called the next day, seeing with astonishment that Juliet's condition had improved, he exclaimed: "Something miraculous has happened here."

A few days later, during her convalescence, the mother asked her daughter for clarification. The little one showed her the painting of Thérèse in front of her bed and said: "She went down from the painting, she gave me a kiss, and then she went up again to the painting." The mother asked her: "Was Sister Thérèse wearing a pretty hat?" "No," Juliet replied, "she was wearing a large black veil." For Mrs. Sompayrac, there was no more doubt: Thérèse really had appeared to her child.

On the following June 11, in spite of the great expense, the family went to Lisieux to give thanks to God. After meeting Mother Agnès of Jesus in the Carmel's parlor, they all went to Thérèse's grave. There Juliet climbed a little wooden bench to grasp an image of her protectress attached to the cross, and kissed it tenderly before putting it back in its place. The family then went to Les Buissonnets and to the Benedictine Abbey of Notre-Dame-du-Pré, where Thérèse had received her first Holy Communion, and concluded their pilgrimage with Mass at Saint-Jacques Church.

At the end of her testimony, the mother explained: "No need to add that our child has been in good health since her miraculous healing. This grace was so striking that my husband, who was neglecting his religious duties, practices his faith again. We trust that the little sister Thérèse will keep protecting us."

HEALED ON THE DAY OF THE RELICS' TRANSLATION

On March 26, 1923, Thérèse's remains were exhumed for their transfer to the newly built shrine in the chapel of the Carmel of Lisieux, in preparation for her beatification on April 29 of that year. Many people had come to attend the event on the city's streets and at the cemetery. Among them, a family from Angers, come to Lisieux at great expense, was watching the gravediggers clearing the vault and taking out the casket of the future Blessed. Their daughter, aged 12, was suffering from Pott's disease, a kind of tuberculosis affecting the backbone. She was brought to the cemetery in a wheelchair, then carried to Thérèse's grave in the arms of her godmother. The gravediggers interrupted their work, letting the woman place the little girl on the ground, only a foot away from the casket. Full of confidence, her godmother fervently prayed to Thérèse, and after a few minutes, the body of the little girl, which was curled up, straightened out: the child got up and walked in front of a crowd of witnesses.

THÉRÈSE OPENS HER APRON AND LETS ROSES FALL

In October 1929, M. L., aged five, was suffering from pneumonia and meningitis. She had a very high fever and no breath was coming out of her mouth: she was dying. On the advice of a friend, her mother knelt at her bedside and implored Saint Thérèse to heal her little daughter, then went out of the room. Left alone, M. L. had a vision: in front of her, as if she were coming out of the wardrobe, a woman dressed as a nun appeared to her, looking like the statue of Thérèse in her village's church. She had a brown apron on her lap. She opened this apron, from which roses began to fall on the side of each arm. The woman was smiling at the child.

The following morning, her relatives, who were prepared for her death, had the village priest come, accompanied by the girl's godfather and the doctor. While the godfather was leaning in to kiss the child, he thought he sensed her breath. A mirror was placed before her mouth and they saw there was a little mist on it. "It's a miracle!" the doctor exclaimed.

Once she was "back to life," the little girl told she had seen a woman who was letting fall roses and roses and roses ... and was smiling at her. The priest immediately understood it was Saint Thérèse of the Child Jesus.

Throughout her life, M. L. had great confidence in Saint Thérèse, to whom she confided her joys as well as her sorrows. Years after being healed, she went to Lisieux on her honeymoon, and subsequently named her only daughter Marie-Thérèse.

HE SPAT OUT THE SWALLOWED PIN

We find in the archives of the Carmel of Lisieux about ten cases of children swallowing a pin (most of the time used to fasten their bib) and spitting it out thanks to the intervention of Thérèse. Several parents even enclosed the pin in their letter as an *ex-voto*. We come across similar cases involving needles, broaches, or varied pieces of jewelry.

In May 1934, in Rio de Janeiro, Brazil, a fifteen-month-old boy swallowed a pin on which medals of the Blessed Virgin and of "Terezinha" were hung. The X-rays showed that the pin, which was open, risked piercing young Paul's mucus membranes.

A neighbor of the family, a pious woman propagating the devotion to Saint Thérèse, advised the mother to pray to the young Carmelite: "You'll see she will rescue your baby," she said to her. A few hours later, the baby spat out the pin without any difficulty, and without after-effects. After examining the X-rays, the doctor explained to the mother that the medal, placing itself in a certain direction, had kept the pin from tearing up the tissue, which greatly surprised him.

A SHOWER OF ROSES AT THE LISIEUX HOSPITAL

In May 1984, N., aged three, was in the hospital in Lisieux. He had undergone a lumbar puncture and could eat nothing. On the following day, his grandparents visited him and joined his mother in the room. Shortly after their arrival, the three of them saw "through the window a wonderful shower of roses falling from the sky." After that, the little boy began to drink. Two days later, he was able to go back home. He was still very weak, "but Little Thérèse had healed him! Without our thinking about it at all," the grandmother wrote. "That is why, dear Mother, I wanted to communicate to you this wonderful story. I have since read several books on Saint Thérèse, and I'm convinced of her great promise [to do good on earth]."

SUFFERING FROM A TUMOR, HER HEALTH CONSIDERABLY IMPROVED

In July 1997, the family of L., aged nine, asked the Carmelites of Lisieux to pray for the little girl, who was suffering from a brain tumor. After undergoing two surgeries to remove 90% of the tumor, she woke up after five days of coma. Shortly after that, she had meningitis and great swelling in her face, leaving her entirely expressionless for three weeks. She couldn't speak anymore and communicated only through a few signs. The surgeon was very guarded on her possibilities of survival, let alone recovery.

Her close relatives rallied around and prayed for her recovery. A relic of Thérèse was placed beside her. After that, L.'s condition got considerably better. The surgeon was "astounded" and didn't understand. She had no memory loss, and the ensuing reeducation enabled her to speak and walk almost normally. While the family was prepared for the possibility of motor disability necessitating the use of a wheelchair, the little girl now jumped rope.

HEALED AFTER THE APPLICATION OF A RELIC

In October 1997, young P., aged eight months, fell ill. Doctors diagnosed her with an ear infection. Her condition rapidly worsened: she was suffering from intermittent fevers, her complexion became greenish, she drank only little bottles of 1 to 1.5 ounces, and didn't sleep anymore.

Her grandmother decided to phone the Carmel of Lisieux, to ask the sisters to pray for her healing. She then went to the bedside of her granddaughter to replace the child's mother, who was going to work. Remaining alone with P., the grandmother prayed and supplicated for her healing, then put on the the sleeping child's chest an image of Saint Thérèse.

In the evening, it seemed to her that she was better. The little one drank a 6-ounce bottle, as she used to do. Shortly afterwards, an appointment was made with a new doctor. He observed that the little girl was in excellent health and that there was nothing the matter with her ears. Her grandmother attributed the healing to Saint Thérèse and gave thanks to the Lord.

A CHILD ADOPTED IN LISIEUX[10]

In 2008, Anne and her husband had been wishing to adopt a child for many years when her brother had just become the proud father of a little girl. In spite of Ann's joy at the prospect of becoming an aunt, this birth was also a trial for her, reminding her that she herself still didn't have a long-desired child.

One day, her mother informed her that she wished to have Mass said for her late parents at Saint-Valéry Chapel. Unable to be there on account of her work, Anne promised to join her in prayer, and went to her neighborhood church. At the end of this Mass, she wanted to light a candle to ask again for the grace of having a child, but didn't know which saint to turn to, having already prayed so much. She finally picked Saint Thérèse.

Two days later, on the feast day of Saint Thérèse, she received a phone call from the social services: a little girl was finally assigned to the couple for adoption! The baby, who was in a children's home in Lisieux, had been born to an unnamed mother[11] two months and fifteen days before: the very day Anne's niece was born!

---

[10] Related in Marie-Martine Muller's chronicle published in *Le Pèlerin*, January 17, 2008.

[11] This refers to the *accouchement sous x* procedure allowed by French law, in which a woman can give birth to a child anonymously, the child subsequently becoming a ward of the nation—trans.

In 1994, to prepare for the 1997 centenary of Thérèse's death, the rector of the Lisieux sanctuary had the idea of sending her relics to the three big French cities she had visited during her pilgrimage to Rome: Paris, Lyon, and Marseille. He then contemplated having them travel to the great capital cities of the five continents, beginning with Europe. Each time, massive crowds made the journey to come and meet Thérèse, and pray to her. Since 1994 the relics have visited more than eighty countries throughout the world. The journey is still going on today, and graces and miracles are obtained through the intercession of the young saint everywhere she goes.

Thérèse's relics in Polynesia

In November 2018, while the relics were in Iceland, Josua Cataño, 13, from Colombia, was healed by Thérèse. The boy had been gravely injured in his left knee after a serious accident while playing soccer. He felt hopeless after his doctor said that he would never be able to play sports again. Josua

[12] Related by Mathilde de Robien in "Là où Thérèse passe, la grâce surabonde" (Where Therese has been, grace overabounds), *Aleteia*, September 30, 2022.

subsequently went with his mother to the Catholic church of Reykjavik, where the relics were exposed.

She related: "Josua cried a lot and implored Saint Thérèse, for he couldn't picture himself not playing soccer. He began to pray intensely to Saint Thérèse and promised her to come and see her at her home, in Lisieux, to bring her flowers and a white candle. He kept praying at home and every Saturday each time he went to the Spanish-language Mass at the cathedral, until the reliquary left Iceland."

Shortly afterwards, Josua went to see the doctor again for a checkup. The latter observed that the knee was entirely healed and was working as if nothing had happened. Josua explained to him that he owed this miraculous healing to the intercession of "that little nun who lives in heaven."

Josua kept his promise: he came to Lisieux with his family to thank Thérèse in May 2019. He met the Carmelite nuns there and gave his testimony during Mass at the basilica: "Saint Thérèse made me the happiest boy of my age. I can play soccer again and that's what matters."[13]

A SQUARE OF CHOCOLATE BROUGHT ABOUT A LIFELONG DEVOTION TO SAINT THÉRÈSE

Children sometimes have unusual requests that get answered. This is the case with Therese Keegan in Ireland, who told her story to the Carmelites many years later, in 2004, when she was eighty.

As early as age four, little Therese Keegan was introduced to Saint Thérèse by her mother. Aged six, the little girl wished

---

[13] Anne Blanchard-Laize, "Guéri après des prières à sainte Thérèse, cet ado colombien vient remercier à Lisieux" (Healed after prayers to Saint Therese, this Columbian teenager comes to Lisieux to give thanks), Ouest France, May 27, 2019.

to purchase a square of chocolate that cost a halfpenny. Since her mother couldn't afford to buy it, the girl asked Thérèse to help her find this sum of money. Dismayed not to find it, she told her: "I won't pray to you any more if I don't find this money after saying one last Hail Mary."

She then knelt down on the sand at the foot of a hill and began to say the Hail Mary. At the moment she was about to say "Holy Mary," she saw something shiny in the sand at a distance. She hurried to the spot and found a whole penny. She dashed off at once to buy her chocolate, forgetting to finish her prayer. Back home, she gave the remaining halfpenny to her mother, telling her that Thérèse had given it for her too. Then, remembering she had not finished her prayer, she told it to her mother who replied: "We will both say a whole Hail Mary after the rosary tonight." The little girl went to bed very happy that night, which represented the beginning of a beautiful friendship with Thérèse.

Little Therese Keegan was not the only one to whom Thérèse did services of a purely material nature. Time and again, she granted temporal and material graces.

Material Assistance

"TRULY, I SAY TO YOU, AS YOU DID IT TO ONE of the least of these my brothers, you did it to me" (Mt 25:40).

The Martin family was a model of Christian charity. In Alençon, Louis and Zélie were in the habit of attending the "Mass of the poor" (so called because it gathered workers and servants who attended it before their day started) early in the morning, at half past five, and would invite the most destitute to dinner and provide them with clothes. Céline Martin said that "extreme charity for his neighbor" was her father's "predominant characteristic."[1] He "always had his hand in his pocket so that he could give something to the beggars he met on the street," and "couldn't see any kind of poverty without relieving it."

As a matter of fact, Louis Martin was a member of several charitable organizations, including the Society of Saint Vincent de Paul, with which he visited the homes of the poor in Alençon. Time and again, he busied himself to assist the poor, to find work for them, or place them in a nursing home. One of his friends, Christophe Desroziers, a French teacher in the Alençon high school, even said at Louis and Zélie's ordinary process that "it is surely from him that his daughters got their noble intentions."

Among Louis's acts of charity, one in particular holds our attention: the assistance provided to a noble family in need, helping the father to find a more profitable position. To thank him, this man's son brought to the Martins' house a

---

[1] Céline Martin, *Mes Saints Parents. Louis et Zélie Martin* (My holy parents. Louis and Zélie Martin) (Paris, Cerf, 2016). All the quotations in this section are from this book.

"prophetic" poem on the occasion of Thérèse's birth: "Smile and grow up quickly / everything is inviting you to happiness: / tender care, tender love... / Yes, smile at the dawn, / O bud that has just blossomed, / Someday you will be a rose..."

As for Zélie Martin, she had beef stew and money regularly sent to families in need in the utmost secrecy through her maid, Louise Marais. By means of this material assistance, she sought to "do good to all spiritually and to bring them a little closer to religious truth and to God's love." Céline added that "she taught her children to give alms to the needy and to respect them."

In her early childhood, during the family's Sunday walks, Thérèse was in charge of giving alms to the poor. Her sisters recounted that she felt respect, tenderness, and "deep compassion" for them. During the ordinary process, Marie said, "it could be felt she was seeing Our Lord in his suffering members." At Les Buissonnets, every Monday, the Martins welcomed the poor, and Thérèse was the one who opened the door to them, to give them bread or money. She also gave to charities the money she kept in her piggy bank, received as a reward for her good grades. At the age of ten, she decided to take care of a poor solitary dying woman, and to bring food supplies and clothes to the mother of a destitute family.

Besides material almsgiving, she also gave the alms of her prayers, as Marie also mentioned. Thérèse related in *The Story of a Soul* her encounter with a crippled old man who, not considering himself poor enough to accept her alms, refused them. Thérèse, then only aged six, said to herself: "I will pray for my poor on the day of my first Holy Communion," which she actually did five years later.

According to the testimony of Mother Agnès at the ordinary process, "Her charity for her neighbor... resulted quite naturally from her charity towards the Lord. She faithfully practiced the divine commandment to love one's neighbor as oneself, and Jesus's new commandment to love him as he himself loves him."

In the archives of the Carmel of Lisieux, we find numerous accounts of material graces received through the intercession of Thérèse. It appears that, just as during her lifetime, she regularly helps those in need, providing them with money, a job, or food.

THE MIRACLE OF THE GALLIPOLI CARMEL

The most famous of Thérèse's "material" miracles is the one that occurred in the Carmel of Gallipoli, Italy, in 1910: through a material grace granted to a poor Carmel, she confirmed that her "Little Way" was sure. As a matter of fact, before her death, she had made this promise to her beloved novice, Sister Marie of the Trinity: "If I am leading you into error with my Little Way of love, do not fear that I will let you follow it for a long time. I will soon appear to you and tell you to take a different route; but if I don't come back, do believe my words are trustworthy: we never have too much confidence in the good God, so powerful and so merciful! We obtain from Him just as much as we hope from Him!"[2]

In January 1910, the Carmel of Gallipoli in Apulia, Italy, found itself in dire straits. The community was very poor and had to settle an important debt to a most insistent creditor. The prioress, Mother Carmela of the Sacred Heart of Jesus, decided to do a triduum in honor of the Holy Trinity, taking as an intercessor Thérèse, whose life the community had read several months prior.

---

[2] *Conseils et Souvenirs de Sœur Marie de la Trinité* (Advice and memories of Sister Marie of the Trinity), https://archives.carmeldelisieux.fr/en/au-carmel-du-temps-de-therese/la-communaute/soeur-marie-de-la-trinite/documents-soeur-marie-de-la-trinite/conseils-et-souvenirs-de-marie-de-la-trinite/.

On the night before January 16, which was the last day of the triduum, at 3 a.m., Mother Carmela, suffering from pleurisy and confined to bed, felt touched by a hand tenderly covering her up to her face with her blanket. Thinking a sister had come out of charity, she said, without opening her eyes: "Leave me alone, it is not a good thing to do, for I am sweating profusely." Presently, a gentle unknown voice replied: "No, my daughter, it is a good thing I am doing." The voice went on: "Listen . . . The Lord uses the inhabitants of heaven as well as those of earth to assist His servants. Here are 500 liras with which you will pay the debt of your community." Mother Carmela replied that the debt was only of 300 liras. The voice replied: "Well, the remainder will be additional. But since you can't keep this money in your cell, come with me." The prioress was wondering how to get up in her condition. Knowing her thoughts, her vision replied: "Bilocation will come to our assistance."

Consequently Mother Carmela went out of her cell "with a young Carmelite nun whose clothes and veil radiated a brightness of paradise that shone a light for [them] on [their] way." This young Carmelite led her to the apartment of the turn,[3] had her open the wooden strongbox where the debt note was kept, and put the 500 liras in it. Mother Carmela prostrated herself before her to thank her and said to her: "*Santa Madre mia!*" (my holy Mother), thinking she was addressing Saint Teresa of Ávila, the reformer of the Carmelite order. The apparition helped her to get up and caressed her affectionately before replying to her: "No, I am not our holy Mother, I am the Servant of God Sister Thérèse of Lisieux. Today is a feast in heaven and on earth! . . . since it is the feast

---

[3] The turn: a room in the outside part of the convent, in which a wooden "turn" made it possible to transfer things into the enclosure—trans.

of the Holy Name of Jesus." Moved and disconcerted, the prioress didn't know what to say and exclaimed: "*Mamma mia!*" So Thérèse put her hand on Mother Carmela's veil "as if to adjust it," gave her a sisterly caress, and then slowly went away. "Wait," Mother Carmela told her, "you might take the wrong way," but with a "celestial smile," Thérèse replied to her: "*No, no, figlia mia, la mia via è sicura, nè l'ho sbagliata!*": "No, no, my daughter, my way is sure, and I was not mistaken!"

After these events, the prioress woke up and, in spite of being exhausted, got out of bed and went down to the choir to attend Mass. Finding her very pale, the two sacristan sisters wanted to send her back to bed and call a doctor. She reassured them by saying "that the impression left by a dream had moved [her] greatly," and proceeded to tell them its substance. The two sisters then suggested that she check the contents of the strongbox in question, but Mother Carmela replied that dreams were not to be believed in, that it was a sin. Faced with their insistence, she yielded and went to open the strongbox: "I actually found in it the miraculous sum of 500 liras!" she wrote in her letter to the Carmel of Lisieux, on February 25, 1910. The sum was divided into ten 50-lira notes.

At the end of January, something else happened: the sister in charge of the convent's savings found an excess of twenty-five liras in the receipts, and couldn't understand the presence of this additional money, for they were in the habit of being thorough with their accounting. The only explanation they found was that Thérèse herself, knowing the great difficulty the monastery still found itself in, put this money at the bottom of the box. At the end of February, March, and April, this occurred again, with a different sum of money each time.

At the end of May, Thérèse appeared again to Mother Carmela. After speaking to her about the spiritual life of the community, she told her: "As a proof that it is really I who brought you the excess of money seen in your various bill settlements, you will find a 50-lira note in the box." She added: "The Word of God does what it says." Once again, the prioress dared not to check the strongbox to verify Thérèse's words. But a few days later, two sisters asked her to open it out of devotion, for they wanted to see the last two miraculous notes. On opening it, they discovered with emotion that there weren't two notes inside but three!

One of the two 50-lira notes brought by Thérèse

In June, the sisters again found an excess of fifty liras. On the night of July 15 to 16, Thérèse favored Mother Carmela with a new apparition on the occasion of her name day (Our Lady of Mount Carmel) and gave her a 5-lira note, which she put at the foot of the Sacred Heart statue. She also promised her to soon bring 500 liras. A few days later, Bishop Müller, the local ordinary, informed of the ongoing miracle, told the sisters that he had lost a 100-lira note while doing the accounting for his clergy, and that he hoped Thérèse would bring it to their house. Well, on August 6, the eve of the bishop's name day, Mother Carmela saw Thérèse again. She was holding a 100-lira note, and told her that "the power of God just as easily takes away or gives in temporal as well as in spiritual matters." The note, found as usual in the strongbox, was sent to the bishop, who immediately sent it back to the Carmel.

That was the last time Thérèse provided the Carmel of Gallipoli with money, for these supernatural events brought to public attention the extreme poverty of the monastery, so that many people sent alms to the Carmelites afterwards. However, it was not the last time Thérèse would appear to Mother Carmela, for on September 5, the eve of her first exhumation, she announced to her that "little more than her bones" would be found and got her to understand that she would continue performing wonders.

Mother Carmela explained about Thérèse's apparitions that "almost every time, she let herself be seen around dawn, during some time of personal prayer. Her face was *very beautiful and bright*; her clothes shone with silver-like transparent light, her *words* sounded like an angelic melody."

After these events, the bishop of Gallipoli could observe the great progress made by the whole community in the spiritual life. For besides the material assistance she was bringing, Thérèse, in each of her apparitions, also talked with the prioress about "spiritual things." So the importance of this miracle mainly lies in the fact that it is viewed by all as confirming Thérèse's Little Way.

TWO NOVICES OBTAINED THEIR DOWRY AND COULD TAKE THEIR VOWS

Sometimes Thérèse doesn't hesitate to use human mediators to answer prayers addressed to her. This is what happened in 1911 in the Carmel of Tiana, Spain. In the end of

July, the prioress of that Carmel wrote to Mother Agnès of Jesus to describe her distress and ask her to pray to Thérèse for assistance. The monastery was short on choir nuns,[4] who numbered only three. Out of the five novices they had received, two could have taken vows for more than six months, but the bishop was refusing, as one of them had no dowry and the other had only half of one. Since the Carmel was poor, the bishop thought he couldn't take the liberty of authorizing two destitute nuns to join it—for back then, in order to become a nun as well as to get married, one had to provide a dowry.

A few days after receiving this letter, Mother Agnès received one from a priest, containing the following words: "Out of devotion to Sister Thérèse, my brother and I wish to pay the dowry of a poor girl and help her to be a Carmelite. We would prefer it to be in Sister Thérèse's very monastery, if it were possible."

Mother Agnès replied to him that the Carmel of Lisieux didn't need any new postulants for the time being, and informed him of the situation of the Spanish monastery. The priest immediately got in touch with this Carmel's prioress and offered to pay the dowries of the two novices. He told her the part played by Thérèse in this story.

In November of the same year, the prioress of the Carmel of Tiana wrote to Lisieux again to inform the sisters that Thérèse not only had helped the two novices to have a dowry, but additionally had provided the monastery with two new donations: the first made it possible to extend the chapel, the second to purchase a bell, since the current one was so small it didn't ring loudly enough to be heard.

---

[4] At the time there was a distinction between choir nuns, who sang the offices in the choir, and converses, in charge of domestic chores.

In 1912, an orphanage in Brest, run by a poor community, had to pay a bill of 551 francs to the baker before the end of the month. "For the first time of [her] life," however, the bookkeeper sister was not able to pay this bill. At the time, she was reading in *Pluie de Roses* the account of the Gallipoli miracle. Finding herself in the same situation, she put Thérèse's portrait in the envelope containing the baker's bill, and put it away in the binder containing bills that remained to be paid. She was in the habit, once the sum had been gathered, of attaching the money to the bill and removing them from the binder so as to put them in a strongbox in a locked wardrobe, the key of which never left her.

She prayed for Thérèse's help in settling her debt, without even asking her for a miracle. She simply hoped for some income from the community's work, or else for a donation. Three days before the due date, driven by some intuition, she opened the wardrobe and the strongbox. She mechanically took the first envelope: inside it was the baker's bill, supposed to be in the binder of the bills owed. The sister related: "I swiftly opened the envelope. . . . What a wonder! Along with this bill, it contained its exact amount, five bills of a hundred francs, another of fifty francs, and a coin of one franc, 551 francs in total! Out of emotion, I burst into tears! Sister Thérèse had renewed for me, unworthy as I was, the Gallipoli miracle!" No natural cause can explain the presence of this money in the strongbox: there had been no income in the meantime, and nobody had access to the strongbox except the bookkeeping sister.

SISTER THÉRÈSE FILLS THE PURSE

Around 1911, a man passed away, leaving his wife and his four children with heavy debts. At the same time the wife was introduced to Thérèse, but didn't think of turning to her. Eighteen months later, remembering the Gallipoli miracle, she decided to invoke Thérèse with all her family. About ten days later, a female relative she barely knew offered to come and live in her house and to pay rent. From that day onward, the family constantly prayed to Thérèse when in financial trouble. One day, finding themselves out of work with only two francs to live on, they received the visit of a relative who left them the sum of ninety francs. The mother consequently got into the habit, when she had run out of money, of putting her purse before the portrait of Thérèse, who filled it every time "in a providential way." Strangely, she observed that the miracle would occur only when they were left with no more than two francs. One of the family's children concluded: "Sister Thérèse probably wants to force us to practice abandonment to divine Providence. What is absolutely certain is that her intercession, so visible and helpful, so deeply touched the heart of my mother that it transformed her, strengthening her faith and restoring her courage."

SHE LOST A COIN AND FOUND IT BACK . . . IN HER HAND!

In 1913, the nuns of the Visitation monastery of Richmond wrote to the Carmel of Lisieux to tell what had happened to one of their pupils, Nellie, aged 15. A recent convert to Catholicism, she was particularly drawn to Thérèse. One day, the superior having asked her to go and do the shopping, Nellie lost a quarter. Quite annoyed, since it had already happened to her once before, she feared being scolded, and even being suspected of theft. She retraced her steps in search of the coin but couldn't find it. She therefore resigned herself to going back to the convent and confessing her sin, but prayed to Thérèse for help. While she was bracing herself for the interview with the superior, "she [felt] the money falling into her hand." She didn't understand where this coin had come from. Nobody could have given it to her, for she was alone at that moment. The money couldn't have been concealed under a glove or a sleeve either, for her hands and wrists were bare. She therefore was persuaded that "only the 'Little Flower' could do it!"

A FAMILY IN DISTRESS IN POLAND

At the beginning of World War I, a completely destitute landowner from the Podolia region (in present western-central Ukraine) sought refuge with his wife, his sister, and his four children in Kraków. With no resources, employment, or connections, they lived in an attic with no heating, at an already very cold time of the year.

In these circumstances, the mother read *The Story of a Soul*, and encouraged her husband and her children to pray to Thérèse. One day, as they took their meager meal, the wistful mother was not eating. Her husband said: "You are not eating? What's on your mind?" She replied: "I'm praying to this little saint whom I love so, Sister Thérèse of the Child Jesus, and I'm begging her to come to our rescue. Let's start a novena in her honor together. I'm sure she will help us." They immediately started the novena.

That very afternoon several women in charge of finding housing for refugees visited them and told them: "We have found you a house and will obtain coal for you." A few hours later, the father met his home region's bishop, who happened to be passing through Kraków. The latter got him a job which guaranteed him a good situation. In one day, Thérèse had provided for all the needs of this family.

HE FOUND A FARM AFTER A PILGRIMAGE TO ALENÇON

In 1921, Louis Lucas, a father of ten children from Plovan, Finistère, forced to leave his farm, was looking for a small sharecrop farm to rent. Because of the rent crisis, however, it was impossible to find one. He had been searching in vain through the whole department, and even a trip to Dordogne had proved unsuccessful. The parish priest of Plovan heard it was possible to find sharecropping in Sarthe, not far from Alençon. On September 28, the two men went there, along with Louis's brother-in-law. Once arrived, they went to Notre-Dame Church, where Thérèse had been baptized, and the priest said Mass "for the intention of obtaining through the intercession of Sister Thérèse the grace of finding a farm for Louis Lucas, who needed it so much." After Mass, they went to Saint-Rigomer-des-Bois, where they were told that changeovers among farmers were not done at that time of year, but at Easter. The disappointed party was on the train back to Brittany when, on the morning of September 30, they were approached by a man who asked if they were coming back from a pilgrimage. They replied: "No sir, we are looking for a sharecrop farm for a large family and haven't found any." Hearing this, the man told them: "Come with me, I have what you need." Astounded, they followed him to the vicinity of Lorient, visited a beautiful sharecrop farm, and very quickly made a deal. At the same time, the wife of the farm owner had gone on a pilgrimage to Lourdes with her daughter to ask for the grace of finding good sharecroppers. Our Lady of Lourdes and Thérèse had therefore joined forces to grant this grace to the two men.

A VIOLIN TO PLAY AT THE EXHUMATION

Miss Blanche Bantignies and the priest she kept house for wished to attend Thérèse's exhumation on March 26, 1923, but the priest was 100 francs short of being able to pay for their journey. Not wishing to go without him, Blanche resigned herself to not going. The day before the big day, a Sunday morning, the mailman brought a letter: one of the priest's relatives was asking him to play a violin piece in honor of his last visit. The priest had not touched his violin for more than one month; on opening his case, much to his surprise, he found inside it an envelope containing 100 francs, one hour before the departure!

Translation of Thérèse's relics from the cemetery to the Carmel on March 26, 1923

MATERIAL ASSISTANCE ON THE OCCASION OF A SOLEMN COMMUNION CEREMONY[5]

In 1923, the Prin family found itself in dire straits after two months of strike at Mr. Prin's workplace. On May 6,

[5] It was customary in France that one year after their first Holy Communion, a new public ceremony of Communion, called Solemn Communion,

the elder daughter was to receive her Solemn Communion and the parents could afford neither to clothe their children nor to pay for food for the occasion. Mrs. Prin consequently put herself under Thérèse's protection. Shortly afterwards, a woman paid for some of the little girl's Communion outfit and another gave money to clothe the two youngest children. Mrs. Prin also asked Thérèse to give her fifty francs to pay for bread on the Communion day. Having heard of the miracles performed by the Blessed, she expected to find that sum of money somewhere in her house's furniture. But she wrote: "I didn't find it my wardrobe, but I got much more than what I had asked for through the inhabitants of the village." Indeed, the following day, people came and brought her thirteen six-pound loaves of bread, jars of jam, peas, cold meats and other sorts of meats, vegetables, ten bundles of wood costing 2,20 francs each, and 32 francs. The family eventually found itself with much more than necessary, and the mother came to the conclusion that "it can be called a miracle."

This is reminiscent of Zélie Martin's gesture on the occasion of Léonie's First Holy Communion. On that day, she bought a white dress for a poor communicant and invited her to the family dinner in the place of honor.

500 FRANCS FOR A YOUTH VACATION CLUB

In 1923, Julie Watine was running a youth vacation club for about a hundred girls. Wishing to provide each of them with the fabric necessary to make a dress and a walk along the seaside, and to give out rewards to the most worthy of them at the end of the month, she needed 500 francs,

would take place for children. It was the occasion of an important family celebration, just like the first Holy Communion—trans.

which she didn't have. She had the idea of writing a brief note: "Blessed Thérèse, send me please 500 francs for the youth club." She put the piece of paper behind the image of Thérèse in a frame, and then waited, full of confidence. After three weeks, her prayer still remained without results. Since the vacation was coming to an end, she pressed Thérèse to intervene rapidly. That very day, Julie's brother announced to her the success of some business deal and informed her he wanted to help the poor. He told her: "I still find myself with the sum of 500 francs; that number is haunting me and I don't know why I feel pressed to give it to you at once." At which point his sister told him about her request to Thérèse. Deeply moved, he commented: "She works wonders." He himself had felt protected during the war while fighting in Verdun, and attributed to Thérèse his coming back unscathed.

THE CZECHOSLOVAKIAN BUTTER SELLER

One day in December 1926 in Jägerndorf, Silesia (now Czechia), Margarete passed by her butter seller around 6 p.m. The latter came to town each Thursday to sell her butter door-to-door. She lived a three-hour walk from Jägerndorf and covered the distance on foot, for the town was not yet served by the railroad. Surprised to see her there so late, Margarete said: "What, you are still in town? My goodness!" The seller replied: "I am quite disheartened, since the morning I've been busy going from house to house but almost no one buys my butter. The evening has come and now I have to go back home. I have had so much trouble and fatigue today, and on top of that I still have a loss of almost 200 korunas. At home my three poor little children are waiting for me, and they are hungry." And she began to sob. Margarete "shared her discouragement, mostly because it was the end of the month and before Christmas," and because she couldn't give 200 korunas to help her.

Back home, Margarete made the following prayer: "Saint Thérèse, I beseech you, listen to me at least this time. You are French, I am German. Our nations don't love each other, I know that, but I love you a great deal, because you loved the good God so much and because you were so kind! You are in the house of God, who is the richest one; tell Him the story of this poor butter woman, pray to Him, so that she can sell her butter and her children can have bread! Fulfilling my request will be your answer; this way you will tell me that you also love the former enemies of your homeland, that you know me, that you know my love, and—forgive my great presumption—that you love me a little too."

The following Thursday she went to meet the butter seller, who told her: "See, ma'am, the other week, when I was so discouraged, a woman suddenly came to me, saying: 'Ah, you still have butter, I was afraid I wouldn't find any.' That woman bought all my remaining butter and promised me to always be my customer." From that day on, each Thursday she sold out all her butter, and this in the span of a few hours only, which allowed her to go back to her children sooner. Informed of Margarete's prayer, she was full of gratitude to the good God and to "her little Thérèse."

A CAR ON SEPTEMBER 30

In September 1983, M., from England, made a novena to Thérèse to be able to buy a car. Shortly afterwards, her parents came and visited her. In the course of a conversation, they told her: "M., you need a car, we are going to buy you one. Look for one." At the end of the month, they gave her a check with which to buy the car she so much needed.

What surprised M. was the coincidence of dates: the car was registered on September 30, 1983, the anniversary of Thérèse's death, and her appointment at the dealer's took place on October 1, the feast day of Thérèse. Moreover, the letters on the license plate corresponded with her initials, her husband's, and those of their children!

"A SISTER CAME ON YOUR BEHALF"

In August 1987, Father Jean C. Craviotti wrote to the Carmel to report an incident that had happened in the town of Adrogué, near Buenos Aires, Argentina. One of his friends, a Mr. Lopez, was forced to retire early due to heart disease. When the administrative procedures were about to come to a successful conclusion, he was asked to bring a document stored in the bank of the Buenos Aires province in Adrogué in order to complete his file. But this bank was in the process of moving into another building, and the archives remaining in the former premises were in disarray: the employees couldn't find the desired document. He was told it would be impossible to look for it before the official opening of the bank's new headquarters at the end of October. Quite distraught, he replied: "But sir, I must live!" "I understand, I'm sorry, but. . ." There was no point in arguing.

Mr. Lopez then turned to Thérèse: "Little Saint Thérèse, help me find that document." He began a first novena that was not successful. On June 9, the anniversary of Therese's Act of Oblation to Merciful Love, he began a second one. On June 12, the bank called him and asked him to come, with no further explanation: "Come, sir; we have good news." He presented himself at the counter and was told:

—Well, my friend! Your nun is quite a character!

—Which nun?

—The one you sent.

—You are quite mistaken, I sent no nun.

—Yes you did! A sister came in your name. She is quite a character, she knows the archives better than I do!

—How so?

—She told me: "Mr Lopez needs the certificate you have in volume 23, on the second-to-last page." Seeing I was hesitating, she insisted: "Do him a favor." I obeyed and searched in the volume she had indicated. "Oh! here is your document. . ." But when I got back to the counter, the nun had disappeared!

When he heard this story, Mr. Lopez understood what had happened. He asked the employee: "What did she look like? Like this?" He pulled from his pocket an image of Thérèse and showed it to her: "Oh! that's it, it was she who came."

Diverse Graces

THÉRÈSE HAS ALSO MANIFESTED HERSELF IN people's lives through sometimes very simple graces, such as obtaining good weather or finding a lost key. But she has also intervened in emergencies. Many people were rescued from grave danger (accident, assault, fire, drowning). She has given comfort in trials as well as spiritual graces. Thérèse is sometimes found in unexpected situations: right in the middle of an ox pasture, on railroads, or else pacing up and down outside a convent. She keeps surprising us and showing us her constant protection, as long as we invoke her with confidence.

HIS MEDAL PREVENTED THE MACHINE FROM CRUSHING HIM

At the age of 18, René Vernier left his parents to work in a factory in Troyes. There he was subjected to the bad influence of his colleagues, who led him astray from his Christian upbringing. Shortly afterwards, he did his military service. At this time he met hospital nuns who treated him for a wound in his hand. They put him back on the right track and introduced him to Thérèse by giving him a medal.

Once demobilized, René went back to his work in the factory. On June 11, 1923, the transmission shaft of a machine in motion hit him violently. Caught by the arm, his upper garments were ripped off in an instant, and he was caught by the machine, the gears of which were about to crush him alive. The medal of Thérèse pinned to his shirt suddenly touched the connecting sleeve of the transmission shaft, which was instantly unscrewed "miraculously, as it were." He observed that "such a thing had never happened" and that his "supervisor and all the witnesses attributed this protection to the little saint, just as [he did himself]."

FATHER PUNTIGAM'S ROSE NOVENA[1]

On December 3, 1925, Father Anton Puntigam, S.J.,[2] began a novena to Thérèse to ask her for an important grace. He recited every day in honor of the Holy Trinity 24 Glory Be's, "to give thanks for all the graces the Most Holy Trinity [granted to Thérèse] during the 24 years of her life." Wondering if Thérèse would obtain for him the desired grace, he dared to ask her for a sign: that he should receive a fresh and blooming rose during the novena. Should that happen, he promised he would publish his testimony and would recommend this "novena of the 24 Glory Be's."

On the third day, a young lady visited him at the office of the International Eucharistic League and offered him a splendid red rose. He asked her in surprise: "But why on earth are you giving me that rose?" She replied: "Today is my birthday, and since I was given roses, I thought I could bring you one and that it would please you." He testified: "Maybe it was by chance, but nobody had ever given me a single rose like that, let alone in the middle of winter while it was snowing."

On December 24 of that year he began a novena to obtain two other graces. During the first he didn't ask for a sign, for he was feeling directly the effect of the prayer, but during the second, he asked for a white rose. And it so happened that Sister Vitalis, a nurse, met him with a small white rose in her hand, telling him: "Here is something from the Little Thérèse, she greets you a thousand times." Once again joyfully

---

[1] After the testimony published in *Der Eucharistische Völkerbund*, February 1926, p. 64.

[2] Father Anton Puntigam (1859–1926), also called Puntigan or Putigan, was the founder of the International Eucharistic League in Austria, of which Saint Thérèse is patron. He was a missionary in Bosnia before World War I, and gave the last rites to Archduke Franz Ferdinand of Austria, assassinated in Sarajevo on June 28, 1914.

surprised, he asked her: "But where have you brought this small rose from?" The sister replied: "I had gone to the chapel where a statue of the saint has been erected and adorned. Quite contrary to my habit, I went close to the small altar and saw this rose fall from it. I wanted to put it back in place, but since I didn't know where it was supposed to be, I thought of bringing it to you."

Father Puntigam concluded: "This is how Saint Thérèse herself sent me the desired sign from her altar. Isn't it charming? Some will say: certainly it was chance; as for me I think I have good reasons to believe the little saint really obtained for me the grace I had asked for. I therefore once again recommend the 24 Glory Be's as a novena in honor of the little Saint Thérèse of the Child Jesus."

Here is the text of the rose novena:

> Most Holy Trinity, Father, Son and Holy Spirit, I thank You for all the favors and graces with which You enriched Your servant Saint Thérèse of the Child Jesus of the Holy Face during the twenty-four years she spent on this earth.
>
> Through the merits of this saint, grant me the grace I ardently desire: . . . , if it is in accordance with Your holy will, and for the good of my soul. Help my faith and my hope, O Saint Thérèse of the Child Jesus of the Holy Face, once again fulfill your promise to spend your heaven doing good on earth, by allowing me to receive a rose as a sign of the grace I wish to obtain.
>
> Recite 24 Glory Be's.
>
> Saint Thérèse of the Child Jesus of the Holy Face, pray for us.

POPE FRANCIS

Pope Francis was well acquainted with this novena, and was also in the habit of asking for a rose as a sign his prayer had really been heard: "When I have a problem," he said, "I ask the saint, not to solve it, but to take it into her hands and help me to accept it. And I always receive a white rose as a sign."[3] He often happened to find a white rose on his desk, and was in the habit of saying: "Well, it seems Saint Thérèse has been here..." But here is an anecdote told by Federico Wals, who is in charge of the press office in the archdiocese of Buenos Aires. When he still was in Argentina, Cardinal Bergoglio was in the habit of going every August 7 to the feast of the shrine of San Cayetano to celebrate a big outdoor Mass and walk for three or four hours to meet the faithful from the city's different districts. During the 2010 celebration, the cardinal was unwell because of some pain in his leg that painkillers couldn't soothe, and that offering Mass only made worse. When the moment for walking arrived, the pain intensified, to the point that he was asking himself if he would be able to go on. So he asked his chauffeur to wait for him at the next intersection. This is when an athletically built man came to meet him and offered him a white rose. Cardinal Bergoglio took the rose and blessed the man without saying a word. When Federico Wals invited him to get into the car, he replied: "No, no, you don't understand: it's the message I've been waiting for. It will be all right now." In the meantime the man with the rose had disappeared, as well as the pain in his leg. The cardinal explained: "That's the presence of the Little Thérèse. Tell our chauffeur to wait for us at the soccer field of Vélez. We will manage." As a matter of fact, the future pope resumed his walk through the ten districts without feeling any pain for the rest of the day.

---

[3] Austen Ivereigh, *The Great Reformer: Francis and the Making of a Radical Pope* (Picador, 2015).

SAVED FROM ELECTROCUTION

On February 5, 1926, in Perchtoldsdorf, near Vienna, Mizzi Chamra started cleaning an electric lamp. She removed the bulb to avoid breaking it. She began her cleaning, thinking the power was cut off, when she suddenly touched the socket. She received a violent electric shock and lost consciousness. Her father being in Vienna at the moment, she was alone at home with her mother. The latter entered the room and found her on the ground, convulsively holding the lamp and the rag soaked with cleaning product. Her cries invoking the Blessed Virgin brought Mizzi back to consciousness. The current's strength, 220 volts, was shaking the whole upper half of her body. Her eyes were closed, her features distorted. Her horrified mother told her: "What's the matter with you? Let go of the lamp!" But she couldn't: her hands, "horribly contracted," were fixed to the lamp, and her mother couldn't pull off her hands either. Feeling she was dying, Mizzi prayed: "Jesus! Jesus!" and then recited the act of contrition. Suddenly an inspiration came to her mother: "Invoke the little Thérèse of the Child Jesus, have confidence, she will help you!" Presently, she cried out: "Saint Thérèse, come to my rescue!"

Here is what happened then: "I instantly felt something inexpressible: it seemed to me she was breaking my bonds herself. The current stopped, my grip relaxed. I was saved! . . . I was left with mere burns, which healed after only six weeks. After two years, the scars are still quite visible—I will probably always have them, as a memory of the protection the dear little saint favored me with in such dreadful danger."

THÉRÈSE STOPS AN OX

On July 28, 1926, in Zdole, Slovenia, Ann was out to draw water. She was crossing the enclosed plot of land in which her brother's cattle were grazing when an ox rushed at her and knocked her over and threw her up in the air with its horns. As passersby came to her rescue, the ox moved away a little. Ann pulled herself together, sitting on the grass, thinking her ordeal was over. But the animal charged again, dragged her another seventeen yards, and threw her up in the air one more time. He was heading towards her again and was about to pierce her with his horns when suddenly Thérèse, clad in white, got between the ox and Ann. The animal suddenly stopped and abandoned his victim, who was the only one seeing the apparition.

Seriously wounded, Ann had internal lesions. She vomited blood for four days. On the fourth night, she implored Thérèse to come to her rescue. At dawn, the latter appeared to her again and told her: "You will heal. As a token of your gratitude, you will decorate the statue of the Blessed Virgin and every Wednesday and Saturday you will light a lamp before her. You will also publish this favor in religious newsletters for the edification of souls. Tomorrow, you will already be able to attend to your duties." Indeed, the following day Ann had recovered, while all the witnesses thought she would not survive.

SAVED FROM A FIRE

On March 28, 1927, at 3 a.m., a fire broke out in Guayaquil, Ecuador, in makeshift bamboo shelters. It very swiftly spread through the whole district. Several families, surprised in their sleep, died in the flames: there were twenty-seven victims in total.

Among those dwelling in these shelters was a Mrs. Franco, accommodated by friends. At the moment, her daughter María Justina was at the bedside of her aunt in the hospital. She had been devoted to Thérèse for a long time. So when she heard her mother was in great danger, her first instinct was to get on her knees before Thérèse's statue. She told her with confidence: "You will be able to manage it... Save my mother!" Dreadfully worried, she couldn't find anything else to say and left it all to Thérèse.

As soon as possible, María Justina went to the scene of the catastrophe and asked the neighbors about her mother. They enquired: "Whose house was she living at?" "At the Garcia's." "Ah well! Poor girl, resign yourself! If she was at the Garcia's, she is certainly dead, nobody was saved, they all burned to death." Shortly afterwards, María Justina came across a Dominican friar who told her: "Are you looking for your mother? Don't worry about her, she's in our church." Delighted to hear that, she dashed away to go and meet her mother, who told her what had happened.

Awakened with a start by the light and the intense heat, Mrs. Franco had rapidly realized the danger. Taking her clothes, she rushed downstairs barefoot towards the exit. There she found herself stuck, since the door was locked and blocked with a big iron bar. Unable to go back upstairs as well, due to blinding and suffocating smoke, she sat on a step, awaiting death.

Suddenly she heard a noise, "like something falling down," and saw something "like a white shadow that took [her] in its arms and left [her] in the street." A few seconds later, the house collapsed, finishing off the six people still inside it. When the firefighters tried to go inside, they saw that the door was still locked and blocked. María Justina was infinitely grateful for this obvious protection from Thérèse, who "managed to rescue her mother" in spite of the locked door.

THE RABBITS DISAPPEARED

In 1929, a Mrs. Querquant found herself in a complicated situation because of rabbits proliferating in her woods and near her lands. They were destroying her crops, while the owners of the woods turned a deaf ear to her complaints. Nearly ruined, she decided to write to the Carmel of Lisieux and ask for relics. The Carmelites sent her a few rose petals and a little bag containing dust from Thérèse's grave. On June 6, she spread this dust at the place where the rabbits were devastating everything and asked Thérèse to protect her crops as well as those of all impacted by the problem. From that day on, the rabbits stopped coming onto her land.

THÉRÈSE ON A SPECIAL MISSION . . . IN CAIRO

In Egypt, in January 1934, a young office employee at the Postal Service Ministry was fired from her job without notice. Her modest salary was providing for her disabled mother and her blind brother. After hearing the awful news, she told no one about it, but went and confided her distress to Thérèse in a Cairo church.

When she came back to the ministry at the end of the morning to get her things, an usher informed her that the minister himself wished to talk to her. Surprised, since he had never addressed her before and barely knew her name, she went to his office apprehensively.

He rebuked her strongly: "Are you Miss X? You had the audacity to discuss a decision I had made by sending me someone to plead your cause: your merits, the fact you have a blind mother and a disabled brother—or the other way round—your discretion, your competence, all of that was expounded to me zealously, in order to make me yield. Well, you should know I hate recommendations. What do you have to say in your defense?"

Appalled, the girl tried to explain herself: "Sir, I didn't say a word about my dismissal. I asked no one to defend me. I don't understand what you mean."

He retorted: "Don't deny it! Your envoy was there, an hour ago; a beautiful young woman, tall, with green eyes. She was wearing a veil, a brown wool habit and a white cloak that was too short."

At this, the employee pulled an image of Thérèse out of her pocket and showed it to the minister, telling him: "I spoke only to this person." "But it was her I saw!" he exclaimed. "That may be, sir. But she died on September 30, 1897, thirty-seven years ago!"

The minister immediately dashed to his anteroom, calling out to his ushers: "This morning, you let in a young lady and saw me escort her to the exit door, didn't you?"

"Sir, no young lady asked to see you. But on your office's doorstep, we saw you, indeed, move aside as if to let someone go out, but you were talking to yourself..."

The girl kept her job.

THE WRITING ON THE PAINTING WAS ERASED

At Christmas 1940, the nursing sisters of Soultzbach-les-Bains, in Haut-Rhin,[4] were offered a painting of Thérèse by three girls of the village. Under the portrait was written in French: *Sainte Thérèse de l'Enfant Jésus* (Saint Thérèse of the Child Jesus). On November 13, 1941, the Germans commanded the inhabitants to get rid of any book written in French or any painting with French words on it. Since the sisters didn't want to part with the painting representing Thérèse, however, they decided to ask their carpenter to

---

[4] A department in Alsace, in eastern France. To understand this story, one must bear in mind that in 1940 the northern half of France was occupied by Nazi Germany—trans.

glue a piece of paper over the writing. Around 7 p.m., Sister Marie-Hortense asked another sister to take it down in order to bring it to the carpenter on the following day. The sister obeyed and, looking at the painting, realized the writing had disappeared. She immediately called Sister Marie-Hortense and told her: "There is nothing on it anymore!" The latter replied: "Are you crazy?" The sister brought her the painting and she in turn could see that the writing had disappeared. Sister Marie-Hortense wrote to the Carmel: "We were so frightened that we couldn't sleep all night. We were elated, but at the same time a little afraid. We already invoked her daily, how much more do we do it now!" Around twenty witnesses could see that the writing was gone. The parish priest as well as the doctor both confirmed this miracle to the Carmel.

THÉRÈSE HELPED A DEPORTED RESISTANCE FIGHTER TO ESCAPE

On October 3, 1944, near Belfort,[5] Théodore Hennequin was arrested by the Gestapo with one of his brothers on the serious charge of joining the French Resistance. The two men were sent to the Dachau concentration camp, and a few weeks later to Auschwitz, before being assigned to the unit of the Jaworzno camp.

On January 17, 1945, as the Russian troops were getting closer, the SS had the camp evacuated. Around 10 p.m., the four thousand prisoners were on their way and began the "march of death" in the snow, at a temperature of minus 75°F, starving, clothed with rags, and protected only by thin blankets. As early as the first night, many men collapsed, chilled to the bone. The weakest ones were executed with a bullet to

---

[5] The Belfort Territory was a small French department created after the rest of the Alsace region was surrendered to Germany in 1871—trans.

the head on the roadside. Three days and three nights long, with neither rest nor food, Théodore Hennequin struggled to keep marching, supporting his debilitated brother. About half their fellow marchers had already been massacred by the SS. At that point, Théodore was thinking of escaping, and informed his brother of it. The latter first emphatically refused to join him, thinking it would be outright suicide, but eventually was persuaded. So Théodore "with all the fervor of his heart" invoked Thérèse, in whom he had always had deep confidence. He wrote: "I now acknowledge my escape project was insane, but—and this is when my story becomes interesting—I maintain it was being dictated to me by a force more powerful than my will. By dint of suffering and praying so much, I had the impression of being free from any earthly contingency. I was talking with my little saint as with a friend, and the voice I was hearing: 'Go, escape,' seemed quite reasonable to me; I had no doubt it was coming directly from heaven, and that I had to obey it."

On January 20, around 8 p.m., while the party was heading for the small town of Tost in Upper Silesia, Théodore caught sight of a forest in the distance, the Pluschnitzer Forest. He saw in it the opportunity for his escape. After assessing the distance from the SS flanking the march, he chose a suitable moment to move out of line and run away with his brother. Lucid enough as a former military man, he fully understood his escape was dangerous, for the forest was made of high and widely spaced bare pines, and the moon shedding light on the snow made it possible to see clearly in the night. In other words, he would be entirely exposed. He related: "But the inner voice was ordering me to flee. It was *absolutely impossible* to resist it! . . . I commended my fate into the hands of the little saint who was calling me and was supporting my unsteady steps." Presently he gave the signal to his brother and dashed towards an embankment. He immediately sank into over two feet of snow. Hearing the SS yell, he started running again towards the woods. After six feet, bullets began to fly around him, one of them piercing his right arm. He tumbled into a hollow. Thinking he was dead, the SS continued on their way.

Once he had pulled himself together, Théodore saw his brother had not followed him. He now found himself alone and wounded, shivering with cold, in the middle of nowhere. He retraced his steps and reached the "monstrous chain of cadavers" left on the edge of the road in order to collect a dozen blankets. He then went into the forest, laid two blankets on the snow, and wrapped the other ones around his feverish body. He wrote: "After that, I offered to God and to my dear saint the most fervent prayer of thanksgiving a man could say, thanking them for allowing me to escape the bullets, and asking them to perform one more miracle on my behalf, so that I would not die in this deserted and unknown forest."

On January 21, around 4 a.m., Théodore got up and walked in a thick fog in search of a shelter. He related: "I think Saint Thérèse must have supported me, for I can't understand today how I was able to walk two hours without falling down." Around 6 p.m., he reached the village of Pluschnitz and asked a farmer for help. The latter first refused to help him out of fear, but his wife let him onto their farm, serving him a hot drink and a piece of bread. After ten minutes they sent him away for fear of being shot. A despondent Théodore set off again in the fog and took refuge for a few hours in a haystack 550 yards away from the village.

On January 22, shortly before dawn, he painfully got up and set off again towards the village center. The fog having dispersed, he caught a glimpse of the church steeple and headed in its direction in the hope of hiding there and waiting for the parish priest. "I knew that in the situation I found myself in, only the Lord could save me. His house, for me, was the ultimate friendly place.... Not for an instant did I doubt that a priest, even a German one, would refuse hospitality to a dying man." Upon arriving there, he realized that the doors were locked. Feeling hopeless and lost, he leaned against the wall, too weak to get back to his haystack: "What was the point? I had better fall there, a stone's throw away from the tabernacle. But once again, I felt an impulse to get up, while the sun was beginning to rise." He walked about fifty yards and reached a large courtyard surrounded by three houses. "This is when another miracle, and quite an obvious one, occurred." He saw a woman carrying a cooking pot going out of one of the houses, and asked her to have mercy on him. Frightened, she let go of her cooking pot with a scream and went back in. She came out again with an old man: it was the priest, and this place was the rectory. The priest and his servant then assisted Théodore: they washed him, nursed him, gave him warm clothes, and burned his striped prisoner uniform. On the same day, around 4 p.m., the Russian troops entered the village: he was saved.

Since he could not be transported, he remained for one week at his hosts' house before being transferred to a Russian hospital and thence to the Polish city of Częstochowa. After three months in the Russian town of Berditchev, he was back in Paris on July 25, 1945. At that point he discovered what had happened to his fellow prisoners: a mile and a half past the spot of his escape, the SS had carried out the general massacre of those marching with him, his brother included. Out of the four thousand initial prisoners, only seven had survived, including Théodore.

Théodore Hennequin gratefully wrote: "I, who had always had such absolute confidence in my 'little Saint Thérèse,' do you think I could simply attribute to chance the fact that I'm still alive today? Don't you believe, on the contrary, that I must see in all that, not only one but several miraculous interventions of her goodness? My grateful heart has already answered these questions. I loudly proclaim, and I always will, that I owe my safety only to the marvelous protection of Saint Thérèse of the Child Jesus. It was she who urged me to flee, after three days of exhausting march, and that, a few kilometers away from the place where the complete massacre of our line would take place. It was she who, on unknown and enemy land, led me straight to the rectory of Pluschnitz. It is to her that my three young children owe the fact they still have their father today! While this account represents one more testimony against Nazi barbarism, I'm anxious that it should above all be a token of deep gratitude towards the little Saint Thérèse of the Child Jesus."

RESCUED FROM ASSAULT

In the spring of 1948, Teresa, 24, was a student at the Academic School of Nursing in Kraków. She lived with her parents and her sister in a second-floor apartment in the suburbs, near several villas. The district was calm, and the family, after experiencing occupation and war, felt safe at last.

To prepare for her examinations, Teresa regularly sequestered herself in a room overlooking an enclosed garden of trees, to study or to rest after her internship. One evening, after a trying day, she fell deeply asleep. In the middle of the night, she suddenly heard "a vigorous, quite distinct whisper, nonetheless uttered in an extremely calm tone," which was telling her: "Open your eyes! Open your eyes!" She reluctantly opened them and saw a man's figure standing in her room's window frame. Thinking she was dreaming, she closed her eyes. The same gentle voice immediately said again: "Open your eyes!" When she did so, she realized the danger she was in, but was not in the least afraid. With astonishment, she noticed that the little framed image of Thérèse, her patron saint, placed on the nightstand near the window, was surrounded by a luminous halo. She related: "The splendor of the supernatural light was accentuating the face and the gentle smile of the saint, which didn't frighten me but helped me gather all my strength for action."

She then decided not to show she was awake, and observed the intruder and his behavior. The figure was still standing in the window frame, ready to attack. An accomplice outside had put a bench under the window so as to more conveniently catch stolen objects. Teresa tried to think of a way out of this situation. The burglar was so close to her that if he had jumped from the window, he would have landed on the bed. She decided to take the matter in hand: she jumped out of bed, grasped a rolling pin that was on a dresser nearby, and heavily hit the window railing. The surprised intruder jumped backwards and took flight with his accomplice as Teresa ran to her parents. Very shocked, she was at first unable to utter a word to explain what had happened. The following morning, the family saw that the fence had been damaged.

It was many years later that Teresa related this story to the Carmel of Lisieux. She wrote: "Many years have passed since that event, but the impression it left is still vivid. I clearly realize it was a true miracle of Saint Thérèse. She rescued me from the assault."

THÉRÈSE MAKES THE TRAIN STOP

In 1957, a priest was called to the bedside of a sick man in Scotland. The journey was not very long by train, but he mistakenly boarded an express train that didn't serve the small village he had to reach. He then began to invoke Thérèse. As the train was drawing near the village in question, though it wasn't meant to stop, it abruptly braked. The priest took advantage of the situation to open his door and jump onto the platform. A station agent came to meet him and mumbled to him: "You'd better keep these nuns in their convents instead of letting them out to stop trains!" The priest immediately understood Thérèse had answered his prayer, and noted that it was the fastest intervention he had ever heard of.

THÉRÈSE ON THE FARM

In 1982, Harry visited some friends on a farm in Shropshire, England. Harold, the farmer, owned a little over eighty cows, not counting heifers and calves. His wife Rosemary helped him on the farm and gave every newborn calf its name. Along the years, Harold had built a good herd that guaranteed them a decent income.

Troubles began very early one morning when Hazelnut, one of his best cows, was found lying in a field, unable to get up for milking. Harold got in touch with the doctor, who rapidly arrived and, upon examination, announced that the cow had a broken hip, which left them no other choice than to slaughter her.

A devastated Harold called a slaughterhouse to have Hazelnut killed the following day, and her carcass removed. He nonetheless asked the veterinarian to send his main partner to check the wound. The cow was worth at least 1,000 pounds sterling, but once dead she would be worth only a few hundred pounds. He didn't want to lose such a good animal and preferred to get a second opinion. The partner, a specialist in cattle diseases, came to the same conclusion, and confirmed it would be charitable to prevent the cow from suffering by killing her as soon as possible.

As a result, Harry turned to Thérèse and asked her to help him, not believing for a moment that his prayer would be answered. He nonetheless gave it a try: "After all, she promised to help those on earth who called upon her." Shortly afterwards, Harold checked on the cow in the field, and to everybody's astonishment, she was standing on four legs, which she had managed without any assistance, mildly limping in the field. Having hastened to call the slaughterhouse to tell it its services were no longer required, he isolated Hazelnut from the herd in a separate field so that she would not be shoved by other animals, and to verify that she could stand. He called the veterinarians again for a consultation. They were rather surprised to see the cow back on her feet, and even more to notice there was no trace of the fracture they had observed and felt. Hazelnut very soon could join the other heifers, giving more milk than any other cow in the herd.

A JOB OFFERED BY MR. ROSE!

In the United States, Mary had received a rose numerous times after praying to Saint Thérèse. In February 1994, she asked for her assistance in order to find a job. Shortly afterwards, she found a rose on her doorstep. In the afternoon, a Mr. Rose called her to offer her a job. "Saint Thérèse really sends signs in the form of roses!" she concluded.

In December 2003, Mr. L. passed away from cancer. His wife had commended him to Thérèse so that his departure might take place painlessly and without a long agony, which had been granted to her. After his death, Mrs. L. continued to pray to Thérèse that she might know if her husband was happy where he was. One evening in February 2004, around seven, she drove to a pizzeria with her daughter, aged 24. When they left the restaurant around nine, her daughter exclaimed: "Look, Mom, your car!" It was covered with fresh rose petals, without leaves or stems, from the front hood to the back by way of the roof. There weren't any on the other cars, parked in front of and behind hers—and none in the gutter or on the road. At that point, Mrs. L. remembered Thérèse's promise to let fall a shower of roses and understood this was the answer to her prayers. Shortly afterwards, she traveled to the basilica of Lisieux to, in turn, offer a bunch of roses to Thérèse in thanksgiving.

In the Carmel
and for Her Relatives[1]

ON JULY 13, 1897, THÉRÈSE TOLD HER THREE sisters: "I can't think much about the happiness that lies in wait for me in heaven; the only expectation that sets my heart racing is the love I will receive and will be able to give. And I also think of all the good I wish to do after my death: to have infants baptized, to help priests, missionaries, the whole Church . . . but above all to comfort my little sisters."

Nonetheless she clarified: "Do not believe that once in heaven I will hand things to you on a silver platter. . . . It is neither what I had myself nor what I wished to have. You may undergo great trials, but I will send you lights that will help you appreciate and embrace them. You will be forced to say, as I did myself: 'Lord, You delight us with all that You do.'"[2]

While Thérèse helped many people around the world, she also manifested herself several times to her Carmelite sisters, to relatives, or to close friends. But as she had announced, she didn't always solve their problems easily. Like everybody else, they had their own share of trials, but Thérèse accompanied them and showed them her presence through little signs that comforted or encouraged them, sometimes continuing her teaching from heaven. Her nearness could be seen in little things of daily life, to which she continued to attach importance as she did in her lifetime.

At the ordinary process in 1910, Mother Agnès of Jesus said that within the convent she did "not observe sensational

---

[1] Unless otherwise specified, this chapter's quotations are taken from the testimonies at the ordinary and apostolic processes.
[2] *Last Conversations.*

healings, but nonetheless a few marvelous events." She particularly mentioned that all the sisters' fervor increased and that they progressed in "their understanding of simplicity and humility, and their love for these virtues," under the influence of her younger sister.

As for Sister Geneviève, she observed that Thérèse, who "said she would take care of [the] novitiate, which was her greenhouse for souls consecrated to Merciful Love . . . sent many recruits to it; but she also called to heaven several of the most deserving ones," in particular Sister Marie of the Eucharist, a cousin of Thérèse and one of her novices, who died quite young from tuberculosis in 1905.

Just as with her loved ones, Thérèse does not necessarily perform great miracles for us today, but she accompanies us in our daily life and manifests herself through little signs, encouraging us to follow her Little Way.

SISTER SAINT VINCENT DE PAUL

Thérèse's first supernatural manifestation in the Carmel took place the very day of her death. Its recipient was Sister Saint Vincent de Paul, a converse nun, despite the fact that this sister had made her suffer much, and had said a few weeks before her death: "I don't know why we make such a big deal about Sister Thérèse, she does nothing remarkable; we don't see her practice virtue, we could not even say she's a good nun." To which Thérèse, who loved humility, had reacted thus: "Ah! to hear on my deathbed that I'm not a good nun, what a joy! Nothing could please me more!"

On the day of Thérèse's death, Sister Saint Vincent de Paul kissed her feet, apologized for her affronts, and beseeched her to heal her of her infirmity, a kind of cerebral anemia she had been suffering from for several years, which prevented her from thinking clearly. That grace was granted to her by Thérèse on that very day.

SISTER MARIE OF THE TRINITY

Having entered the Carmel of Lisieux on June 16, 1894, after a first attempt in the Carmel on Avenue de Messine in Paris, Sister Marie of the Trinity was for three years Thérèse's youngest novice, and her fervent disciple. The writings she left enable us to discover what Thérèse taught her novices.

Sister Marie of the Trinity and Thérèse

THÉRÈSE DID NOT LET GO OF THE ROSARY

The day after her death, according to custom, Thérèse's body was exhibited at the choir grille of the Carmel's chapel. Carmelite nuns being considered holy women, many people were in the habit of bringing objects of piety to have them touch the body. A Carmelite was tasked with taking the objects through the grille and putting them for a moment on the deceased sister.

When Thérèse died, Sister Marie of the Trinity was entrusted with this duty. She was touching a rosary to the body, when an extraordinary event took place: "Contrary to what the Servant of God had asked me,[3] I was crying unceasingly and could not console myself on her death. Well, when I got closer to her so as to have her touch a rosary someone had just handed on to me, she started to hold tight to it. Very gently, I lifted her fingers to take it back; but every time I removed it from one finger, it was immediately taken back by another finger. I did it again five or six times, to no avail. My little sister Thérèse was telling me inwardly: 'As long as you will not show me a smile, I will not give it back to you.' As for me, I kept replying to her: 'No, I'm too upset, I prefer to cry.' People at the grille, however, were wondering why on earth I was taking so much time (it had been going on for maybe five minutes); I was quite embarrassed about it and begged my little Thérèse to let me take back the rosary; I even pulled it to have it by force, to no avail; it was as if she had iron fingers to hold it, and yet

---

[3] Eight days before her death, Thérèse had said to Sister Marie of the Trinity: "Why cry over my death? What completely useless tears! You would be crying over my happiness! Anyway, I pity your weakness and allow you to cry on the first days" (*Conseils et Souvenirs de Sœur Marie de la Trinité*).

her fingers had remained very supple. In the end, unable to take this anymore, I began to smile.... It was what she wanted, for she immediately let go of the rosary, and it was in my hands without my having to pull it."

THE UNSTITCHED PLEAT

The following day, Sister Marie of the Trinity received another nod from Thérèse, but the story had begun a few days before. For convenience's sake, the young novice had made a large pleat in her robe, solidly stitched so that she would not be forced to make it again every morning when putting on her cincture. It was contrary to monastic customs, however, and Thérèse had told her to unstitch it; Marie of the Trinity didn't do so immediately, for she couldn't bring herself to.

In Carmelite life, little things are of great importance, and while it can be tempting to come up with apparently insignificant little adjustments to make one's life easier, these nonetheless say a lot about one's spirit of obedience. Thérèse paid great attention to fidelity in little things, and she was uncompromising with her novices on the subject.

After Thérèse's death, having a guilty conscience because of this pleat, Marie of the Trinity said to herself: "She sees that I still have it, and perhaps it saddens her?" She then said the following prayer: "Dear little sister, if this pleat displeases you, unmake it yourself, and I promise not to make it again." And the very next day, she saw with both fright and consolation that the pleat was entirely unstitched and that there remained no trace of the thread. "It was a warning to me to thoroughly put into practice all her advice and recommendations," she concluded in her testimony at the ordinary process.

A HEALING ENABLING HER TO FOLLOW THE RULE

In 1909, Marie of the Trinity had been suffering from stomach distension for more than two years. No medicine had been able to heal her, and her condition was gradually worsening. She was worried at the prospect of no longer being able to follow the austere rule because of this illness. "In [her] distress and full of faith," she decided to anoint her stomach with the oil burning before the statue of the Virgin of the Smile. She beseeched Thérèse to have mercy and to heal her so that she could follow the rule. "All trace of disease disappeared immediately, and this grace has been extended to this day, March 15, 1911."

GRACES FOR HER FAMILY

Marie of the Trinity also attributed to Thérèse several graces received by her family. She was especially certain her mistress of novices had comforted her parents at the hour of their death. Some of her father's last words demonstrated it: "I don't need anything, I'm in the company of little sister Thérèse."

She also attributed to her the "complete and quite necessary conversion of [her] younger sister, as well as her vocation to Carmel." The latter, after a novena to Thérèse, wrote: "I cannot believe in my own change; even if I wanted to live in indifference as before, I could not. And to think it all came after a novena to Sister Thérèse of the Child Jesus! Little by little I have come to love the good God and to feel loved by Him; here lies all the mystery of my conversion."

SISTER JEANNE-MARIE OF THE CHILD JESUS

One of the Lisieux Carmelites who most benefited from Thérèse's graces was Sister Jeanne-Marie of the Child Jesus, a converse nun who, however, entered the Carmel only after

Thérèse's death, in 1905. But she always had great devotion to her, invoking her frequently while she was working to ask for her assistance or for "the grace to carry out without ever complaining all that is asked of her, even additional work."

THE WATER TANK FILLS UP BY ITSELF

Sister Jeanne-Marie worked in the kitchen with Sister Marie-Madeleine, a former novice of Thérèse. On February 23, 1910, around 4 p.m., while the head cook had been busy cleaning the windows on a ladder for some time, her assistant was about to fill the water tank of the kitchen's kettle, which contained four big jugfuls of water—17 gallons. Sister Jeanne-Marie's first reaction, being tired from her own work, was to say to herself: "Ah well! I will let her do it, I have too much to do." Then, seeing her companion also was tired, she gathered her courage and eventually offered to help her with her difficult task, "thinking that this way she was imitating the attentive charity of Sister Thérèse of the Child Jesus." She then told Thérèse: "Dear little sister, help me, please."

After cleaning and wiping down the tank, she poured into it the content of a first jug located near the furnace, then joined Sister Marie-Madeleine who had gone to the water pump to fill a second one. She took this second jug and went back to the tank. On arriving there, she realized it was full! She called Sister Marie-Madeleine: "Oh, come, sister, come quickly! The kettle contains four jugfuls of water—I poured only one into it and it is full! What does it mean? My goodness, I don't understand! Did you fill it?" Marie-Madeleine replied: "But I've only been there a minute, don't you see? I pumped only one jugful. Why, it's extraordinary!" The two sisters came to the conclusion that "the good God sent an angel, and this angel is our dear little Thérèse. She loved charity so much! We wanted to help each other charitably; our little sister in heaven did everything."

THE BOX FILLED UP WITH "CUT AUTHENTICS"

In the week of Christmas 1910, Sister Jeanne-Marie was tasked with making little bags and images with relics to be sent.[4] She had to affix to each the printed seal of the vice-postulator of the cause, which is called an "authentic."

While she was working, she confided to Thérèse her fear of lacking time to finish, and asked her to help. She was particularly worried about the small number of authentics remaining in her box: around a hundred, while she would have needed 900 to 1,000. At 10 a.m., she went downstairs to work in the kitchen. When she came back around 3 p.m., she found the box full with around 800 to 900 cut authentics. Thinking one of the sisters had wanted to do her a service by cutting them, she asked every one of them, but none of them had done it.

When she related this fact to Mother Agnès, the latter was convinced that Thérèse had performed this little miracle, which would be confirmed: "Thérèse herself... completely convinced me of it by making me smell no less than three times a strong scent of fragrant violet while I was recounting this little event to our Reverend Mother."

PERFUME SCENTS

Therese manifested her presence several times to her Carmelite sisters through naturally inexplicable perfumes. Rose, violet, mock orange, heliotrope, incense—the scents were diverse but always strong. In their testimonies, the sisters

---

[4] In these little bags or on these images could be found fabric that had touched Thérèse, wood from the infirmary's floorboard or from her cell, or dust from her grave, for instance.

who had experienced it explained that these scents always turned up when they didn't expect it, mostly after an act of obedience or charity, or sometimes with the purpose of consoling or encouraging them. The scent vanished as soon as the person who was favored with it understood that Thérèse was manifesting herself to her. It never came when the person wished or expected to smell it. For example, on the day of Thérèse's exhumation, September 6, 1910, nobody smelled perfumes emanating from the intact lid of the casket or from the remaining pieces of clothes brought to the community.

This phenomenon began just after Thérèse's death; it occurred on rare occasions for eleven years, before becoming frequent starting in 1908. At first skeptical, Thérèse's sisters feared they were illusions. Mother Agnès of Jesus, as the prioress, deliberately paid little attention to her sisters' claims on this subject. But she herself would be favored with the phenomenon ten times, Sister Geneviève fifteen times, and Sister Marie of the Sacred Heart four or five times. Sister Geneviève began to believe in it when, on entering her cell, the very cell Thérèse had lived in before her, she smelled a scent of roses in the oratory in front of the entrance. Still incredulous, she went out, and on arriving near the staircase at the end of the corridor, she smelled something "like a breath entirely made of rose perfume. I then believed and wanted to thank my Thérèse, but everything vanished immediately."

The first to smell a perfume was Sister Marie of Saint Joseph. In 1896, Thérèse had helped this sister, suffering from bipolar disorder and not easy to be with, in the laundry. Shortly before Thérèse's death, in September 1897, Marie of Saint Joseph picked a violet for her, but she had to be content with "simply slipping it on the windowsill in passing, for it was forbidden to enter the infirmary." Thérèse thanked her in a very particular way the evening of October 1, the day after her death: when she entered her cell, Sister Marie of Saint Joseph found it entirely filled with violet fragrance. Looking everywhere to find where the fragrance was coming from, she found no flowers that could explain it. Suddenly she remembered the little violet of September 13 and understood. The perfume immediately vanished.

Around the end of October 1908, Sister Marthe of Jesus, a converse nun close to Thérèse, went to the laundry room, feeling the urge to perform an act of charity. As she was passing under the cloister, close to the statue of the Child Jesus that Thérèse loved, she perceived a very strong perfume of heliotrope, which she smelled again the next time she passed it, and pointed out to the prioress at the time, Mother Marie-Ange.

Sister Marie of the Trinity was favored several times by perfumes: a scent of violet after performing an act of humility, a scent of roses on opening a closet containing books and images that had belonged to Thérèse, or a scent of incense when she was on her way to do a service. She was also one of the three sisters, along with Sister Marie of the Child Jesus and Sister Thérèse of Saint Augustine, to have smelled a scent of incense near a wooden board. On her way to fetch a parcel by the extern sisters' quarters, Marie of the Trinity saw on the table a moist and worm-eaten board, the origin of which she didn't know. She then smelled "a very strong and delightful scent of incense." She immediately went and informed Mother Agnès of Jesus, and came back with her and a novice. Mother Agnès smelled nothing; as for the novice, she recognized the scent of incense. Mother Agnès then fetched another sister without explaining the situation to her. On arriving, Sister Thérèse of Saint Augustine also smelled the scent. But this scent would be perceived by no other sister when the board was shown to the community during recreation. Told in advance about the phenomenon, the sisters subsequently smelled only moisture and mold. Doctor La Néele, the husband of Thérèse's cousin, then recognized this board as a piece that had come off the casket's front during the exhumation of September 6, 1910, in which he had taken part as an expert. The extern sisters would eventually hear that a worker from the cemetery had deliberately put this piece of wood aside and hidden it in the bushes in order to retrieve it later for his personal devotion.

Sister Marie of the Sacred Heart smelled a very sweet scent of flowers for the first time when passing near the statue of the Child Jesus that Thérèse loved, on her way to the oratory of the Blessed Virgin, where she was going to do a novena for the intentions of people commending themselves to Thérèse. Another time, while she was working with Mother Agnès and another sister, they all smelled a scent of incense. Sister Marie of the Sacred Heart testified having smelled "a penetrating scent of flowers of all kinds that followed [her] to [her] cell" after "performing an act of obedience and charity that cost a lot."

As for Sister Geneviève, she related three particular occurrences of this phenomenon. In March and April 1911, she smelled a "delightful scent of iris roots" emanating from a bag containing dust from under Thérèse's first casket. On February 5, 1912, the anniversary of her investiture and the day the file of the diocesan process for Thérèse's cause was handed over to Rome, she was awakened by a very strong scent of mock orange. Lastly, on March 17, 1915, the day the apostolic process was opened, which was also the anniversary of Sister Geneviève taking the black veil,[5] she found her cell filled with a rose fragrance.

---

[5] After the profession of her solemn vows, which took place in the privacy of the enclosure, a Carmelite nun would receive the black veil a few days

Outside the Carmel, Léonie Martin, Thérèse's sister who was a nun in the Visitation of Caen, also smelled a scent of roses two or three times on September 30, the anniversary of Thérèse's death, around 1910.

SISTER SAINT JEAN BAPTISTE

Around 1907, Sister Saint Jean Baptiste was making little bags with reminders of Thérèse during the time of the great silence.[6] At some point she realized her gas lamp was about to go out. As it was forbidden to fill the gas lamps at night due to the risk of explosion, Sister Saint Jean Baptiste, sorry not to be able to finish her work, invoked Thérèse. "The flame was immediately rekindled and stayed lit the entire hour."

Ten years later, the same sister suddenly passed away. After losing consciousness, she didn't regain it a single time until her death. Mother Agnès then wrote to her sister Léonie: "A little sister of the white veil who was watching over her after her death inwardly asked our little Thérèse if in spite of all she had come to meet Sister Saint Jean Baptiste and had helped her cross the gate of eternal life. At the same instant, she smelled a scent of roses that another sister also smelled. It was a beautiful answer, wasn't it?"

SISTER MARIE-MADELEINE OF THE BLESSED SACRAMENT

According to Sister Geneviève, one of the most remarkable things that happened in the Carmel through the intercession of Thérèse was the healing in 1908 of Sister Marie-Madeleine of the Blessed Sacrament, who was suffering from furunculosis.

---

later during a public ceremony as a symbol of her lifelong commitment to the Carmelite life—trans.

[6] The great silence in a monastery is the period of the day, from compline to prime of the following day, when strict silence is mandatory—trans.

She had been in the infirmary for eight months, one of her legs being infected with "an uninterrupted series of abscesses and furuncles (thirty-five in eight months)." Over the course of May, Mother Marie-Ange suggested that Sister Marie-Madeleine invoke Thérèse, to ask her to be able to resume her work in the kitchen, for she was a converse sister. A first novena was made, during which the illness got worse. A second novena was begun, and at the same time it was decided to apply on the leg of the sick sister a parlor veil[7] which Sister Genevieve thought (without certainty) had been worn by Thérèse. The sister recovered from her illness, which made it possible to identify the origin of the parlor veil without a doubt.

SISTER GENEVIÈVE OF THE HOLY FACE

Céline was the seventh child of the Martins. Thérèse considered her "the little companion of [her] childhood." Having remained "in the world" longer than her sisters, she entered the Carmel on September 14, 1894. She had cared for her father till the end of his life. She was trained as a novice under the direction of Thérèse. We owe to her, a photographer and a painter, the majority of the pictures of Thérèse, as well as her official portraits.

Interior graces

Here are a few accounts of graces received by Sister Geneviève, as related in her testimony at the ordinary process.

"In the first months that followed the death of the Servant of God, I received great interior lights often accompanied with sensible graces. The most important, if not regarding the sensible sign at least regarding the intensity of the interior graces,

---

[7] The large black veil a Carmelite nun put before over face when meeting visitors—trans.

took place in October 1897, only two weeks after the death of my beloved sister. It was on the eve of the feast of the Maternity of the Blessed Virgin Mary; I was praying the Stations of the Cross in the cloister. I suddenly saw a flame that seemed to be coming from the depth of the sky. At the same instant I experienced a supernatural and exclaimed: 'It is Thérèse!' The interior grace surpassed by far what I could express. It is one of the greatest graces I have ever received. In a flash I had the answer to difficulties that had saddened my heart so many times. All my vain worries vanished; Thérèse's 'Little Way' of confidence, abandonment, humility, and spiritual childhood were explained to me and became luminous to my soul."

Sister Geneviève of the Holy Face

"One day a sister had taken from me an object I needed, and I was about to demand it from her somewhat vehemently, when I distinctly heard these words: 'Very humbly!' I recognized Thérèse's voice, and my heart was immediately transformed and inclined to humility."

In a letter to Léonie dated March 23, 1913, Céline related an event that took place on Holy Saturday. The candle this account refers to is still kept in the Carmel.

"I also wanted to share with you a little thing that happened to me yesterday evening, and struck me greatly. I was setting up for solemn adorning in the oratory of the Blessed Virgin near Thérèse's cell. In that oratory are light-bearing angels on two columns. Perched on a chair, I was arranging the candles on the candelabras, the arms of which were all crooked, for they have rather fragile frameworks, and it takes pressure from the thumb almost every time to straighten them up. I still had to tend to one candle, the most difficult to arrange, when the compline bell rang.[8] I was holding the candle, the gilded arm was in my hands, it was not going to be long, and I had so much to do afterwards, it would remain on my mind, I would perhaps forget to do it. In short, I was finding a thousand reasons to get done with it, when I said to myself: 'After all, no! I will offer up this satisfaction to the good God, and anyway it's more in accordance with the Rule . . .' I jumped off my chair, which I left there as a reminder for later. What a surprise! When I came back to the oratory I saw the candle straightened up! . . . I couldn't believe my eyes . . .

"The gilded arm had been moved apart from the shaft in the middle, the candle was as straight as a plumb line; only the small slot in which the candle fits remained tilted because the screw itself is. Our Mother wants me to keep this candle, she says it was Thérèse who fixed it; as for me, I resolved to be even more committed to following the rule,

---

[8] A Carmelite had to stop all activities when she heard the sound of the bell.

since the good God rewards it to such an extent. These little things probably please Him much. It also strikes me to see we live so much in the supernatural world that our smallest acts are seen and known, that they arouse interest in the other world.... O my Léonie, how I am going to do my utmost to never let any of these little sacrifices slip, so as to live from love in order to deserve to die of love...

"We gathered evidence of the fact that no one had touched my oratory."

SISTER FRANÇOISE-THÉRÈSE (LÉONIE MARTIN)

Carmelite nuns are not the only ones to have benefited from favors granted by Thérèse. Her sister Léonie, a nun in the Visitation of Caen, related a beautiful grace in her testimony at the apostolic process: "Around 1900, on a winter evening, overwhelmed by boredom and disgust, I was wearily reciting the Divine Office. That was when a luminous image, by which I was dazzled, appeared on my book of hours. I was not frightened by it, quite the contrary. After an instant I realized this luminous image was a hand. I firmly believed it was my little Thérèse; I was perfectly consoled and felt delightful peace."

CÉLINE GUÉRIN

Jeanne La Néele, Thérèse's cousin, attributed to her intercession "the unexpected peace and calm in which Céline Guérin, [her] mother, died," on February 13, 1900. During her last illness, the latter even admitted: "I am suffering a lot, that is true, but I feel my little Thérèse nearby, quite close to me; her presence gives me courage, it helps me to bear my sufferings." She who had dreaded death eventually approached it with great abandonment to God.

First the spiritual director of Marie Martin, then of the whole family, Father Almire Pichon, S.J., met Thérèse for the first time in 1883. He was preaching a retreat to the Carmelite community in 1888 for the fiftieth anniversary of the convent's foundation. On this occasion, Thérèse, then a postulant, confided her scruples to him in the confessional. He affirmed to her: "In the presence of the good God, of the Blessed Virgin, and of all the saints, I declare you have never committed a single mortal sin."[9]

Father Pichon obtained two healings through Thérèse's intercession. The first took place on January 2, 1909. Bedridden because of a fracture in his leg made worse by a new accident, he suffered from copious suppuration for seven weeks, with no hope of healing. He commended himself to Thérèse and on the fifth day of his novena, the wound was totally healed, with no trace of suppuration. "From that moment on I could say Holy Mass again, much to the surprise of the doctor, who had prescribed no other medicine than bed rest," he said.

A few months later, on August 28, 1909, he contracted infectious bronchopneumonia while preaching a retreat to the Augustinian nuns of Paris. The victim of a very severe case, he was considered lost by the doctors, who counseled him to receive the last rites. He then decided to invoke Thérèse again. The nuns who were nursing him joined his prayer. He related: "I was naively telling her to be obedient in heaven as she had been on earth; that if it was God's glory, she might obtain for me simple and rapid healing, but without too sensational a miracle, which is a difficult

---

[9] *The Story of a Soul.*

burden to carry. Well, on the sixth or seventh day, I was able to say Mass. As early as the second day, the doctor told me: 'I don't understand, there must be a saint behind it.' 'Yes, a woman saint!'" At the end of his convalescence, when he thanked the doctor for saving his life, the latter replied: "I am quite innocent of it; you undermined all our ideas about pathology; medically, to us, you were dead."

Conclusion

WHEN WE READ THE ACCOUNTS OF ALL THESE miracles and graces, which are only a tiny fraction of what is kept in the archives of the Carmel of Lisieux, we can see that Thérèse kept her promise to "do good on earth," and that she has not remained idle since 1897.

The day after Thérèse's canonization in 1925, Pope Pius XI said to the French pilgrims: "How powerful her intercession is! What can you not hope for from this saint who promised a 'shower of roses'?"

The sensational miracles of the first years that contributed to her fame and to the flourishing of devotion to her were succeeded by graces that were perhaps simpler, but reveal to us that we are not alone, and that Thérèse accompanies us in everyday life.

If we sometimes have the impression that our prayers are not heard, let us remember the parable of the persistent widow in the Gospel according to Saint Luke, in which Jesus encourages his disciples to "always pray and not lose heart":

"And he told them a parable, to the effect that they ought always to pray and not lose heart. He said, 'In a certain city there was a judge who neither feared God nor regarded man; and there was a widow in that city who kept coming to him and saying, "Vindicate me against my adversary." For a while he refused; but afterward he said to himself, "Though I neither fear God nor regard man, yet because this widow bothers me, I will vindicate her, or she will wear me out by her continual coming."' And the Lord said, 'Hear what the unrighteous judge says. And will not God vindicate His elect, who cry to Him day and night? Will He delay long over them? I tell you, He will vindicate them speedily.

Nevertheless, when the Son of man comes, will he find faith on earth?'" (Lk 18:1–8).

Faith and confidence, indeed, are quite necessary when we pray. Thérèse told her sister Céline: "Let us not tire of praying; confidence works miracles."[1] Indeed, what emerges from the testimonies included in this book is the great confidence and the fervor with which Thérèse was invoked by those whose prayers were answered. A nun testified in 1967 in the *Annales de Sainte Thérèse*: "Saint Thérèse always answers, as long as we have total confidence and make daily efforts in the life of love."

And if we don't know how to address Thérèse when asking her for graces, let us remember that she didn't recite ready-made prayers but talked to God directly, using her own words: "I do as children who can't read do, I simply tell the good God what I want to tell Him, without flowery sentences, and He always understands me.... For me, prayer is a surge of the heart, it is a simple glance cast towards heaven, it is a cry of gratitude and love in the midst of trials as well as of joy; in short, it is something great, supernatural, that dilates my heart and unites me to Jesus."[2]

The answer to our prayers sometimes isn't that we had hoped for, but as Thérèse said to her sister Léonie: "The only happiness on earth is to endeavor to always find delightful the lot Jesus gives us."[3]

"EVERYTHING
IS GRACE."[4]

---

[1] Letter of July 8, 1891.
[2] *The Story of a Soul.*
[3] Letter of July 17, 1897.
[4] *Last Conversations.*

174

ACKNOWLEDGMENTS

I first would like to thank Bishop Jacques Habert, bishop of Bayeux and Lisieux, for reading this work and agreeing to write a preface.

I also thank Sister Francine, prioress of the Carmel of Lisieux, for her confidence, and for authorizing me to search the Carmel's archives.

Thank you also to the whole community of Lisieux, and in particular to Sister Marie-Bernard for her proofreading and her prayers.

I am also grateful to Hélène Mongin, my publisher, who invited me to write this book, for her advice and her proofreading, as well as for our agreeable collaboration.

Finally, let me thank Isabelle and Nicolas Burette for their careful proofreading.

A CALL TO GIVE TESTIMONY

If you wish to give your testimony about graces received through Thérèse's intercession, you too can write to:

Archives du Carmel de Lisieux
37, rue du Carmel
F-14100 Lisieux
FRANCE

www.ingramcontent.com/pod-product-compliance
Lightning Source LLC
Chambersburg PA
CBHW022020090426
42739CB00006BA/222